www.EffortlessMath.com

... So Much More Online!

✓ FREE Math lessons

✓ More Math learning books!

✓ Mathematics Worksheets

✓ Online Math Tutors

Need a PDF version of this book?

Please visit www.EffortlessMath.com

5 Full-Length ISEE Upper Level Math Practice Tests

The Practice You Need to Ace the ISEE Upper Level Math Test

By

Reza Nazari & Ava Ross

All inquiries should be addressed to:

info@EffortlessMath.com

www.EffortlessMath.com

ISBN: 978-1-64612-200-4

Published by: Effortless Math Education

www.EffortlessMath.com

Description

5 Full-Length ISEE Upper Level Math Practice Tests, which reflects the 2019 and 2020 test guidelines and topics, is designed to help you hone your math skills, overcome your exam anxiety, and boost your confidence -- and do your best to ace the ISEE Upper Level Math Test. The realistic and full-length ISEE Upper Level Math tests show you how the test is structured and what math topics you need to master. The practice test questions are followed by answer explanations to help you find your weak areas, learn from your mistakes, and raise your ISEE Upper Level Math score.

The surest way to succeed on ISEE Upper Level Math Test is with intensive practice in every math topic tested-- and that's what you will get in *5 Full-Length ISEE Upper Level Math Practice Tests*. This ISEE Upper Level Math new edition has been updated to replicate questions appearing on the most recent ISEE Upper Level Math tests. This is a precious learning tool for ISEE Upper Level Math test takers who need extra practice in math to improve their ISEE Math score. After taking the ISEE Math practice tests in this book, you will have solid foundation and adequate practice that is necessary to succeed on the ISEE Upper Level Math test. **This book is your ticket to ace the ISEE Upper Level Math!**

5 Full-Length ISEE Upper Level Math Practice Tests contains many exciting and unique features to help you improve your test scores, including:

- Content 100% aligned with the 2019 - 2020 ISEE Upper Level test

- Written by ISEE Math tutors and test experts

- Complete coverage of all ISEE Upper Level Math concepts and topics which you will be tested

- Detailed answers and explanations for every ISEE Upper Level Math practice questions to help you learn from your mistakes

- 5 full-length practice tests (featuring new question types) with detailed answers

This ISEE Upper Level Math book and other Effortless Math Education books are used by thousands of students each year to help them review core content areas, brush-up in math, discover their strengths and weaknesses, and achieve their best scores on the ISEE Upper Level test.

About the Author

Reza Nazari is the author of more than 100 Math learning books including:
– **Math and Critical Thinking Challenges:** For the Middle and High School Student
– **GED Math in 30 Days**
– **ASVAB Math Workbook 2018 - 2019**
– **Effortless Math Education Workbooks**
– **and many more Mathematics books …**

Reza is also an experienced Math instructor and a test–prep expert who has been tutoring students since 2008. Reza is the founder of Effortless Math Education, a tutoring company that has helped many students raise their standardized test scores—and attend the colleges of their dreams. Reza provides an individualized custom learning plan and the personalized attention that makes a difference in how students view math.

You can contact Reza via email at:
reza@EffortlessMath.com

Find Reza's professional profile at:
goo.gl/zoC9rJ

Contents

ISEE Upper Level Test Review

The Independent School Entrance Exam (ISEE) is a standardized test developed by the Educational Records Bureau for its member schools as part of their admission process.

There are currently four Levels of the ISEE:

- ✓ Primary Level (entering Grades 2 - 4)
- ✓ Lower Level (entering Grades 5 and 6)
- ✓ Middle Level (entering Grades 7 and 8)
- ✓ Upper Level (entering Grades 9 - 12)

There are five sections on the ISEE Upper Level Test:

- o Verbal Reasoning
- o Quantitative Reasoning
- o Reading Comprehension
- o Mathematics Achievement
- o and a 30-minute essay

ISEE Upper Level tests use a multiple-choice format and contain two Mathematics sections:

Quantitative Reasoning

There are 37 questions in the Quantitative Reasoning section and students have 35 minutes to answer the questions. This section contains word problems and quantitative comparisons. The word problems require either no calculation or simple calculation. The quantitative comparison items present two quantities, (A) and (B), and the student needs to select one of the following four answer choices:

(A) The quantity in Column A is greater.

(B) The quantity in Column B is greater.

(C) The two quantities are equal.

(D) The relationship cannot be determined from the information given.

Mathematics Achievement

There are 47 questions in the Mathematics Achievement section and students have 40 minutes to answer the questions. Mathematics Achievement measures students' knowledge of Mathematics requiring one or more steps in calculating the answer.

In this book, there are five complete ISEE Upper Level Quantitative Reasoning and Mathematics Achievement Tests. Let your student take these tests to see what score they will be able to receive on a real ISEE Upper Level test.

Good luck!

Time to Test

Time to refine your skill with a practice examination

Take practice ISEE Upper Level Math Tests to simulate the test day experience. After you've finished, score your tests using the answer keys.

Before You Start

- You'll need a pencil and a timer to take the test.

- For each question, there are four possible answers. Choose which one is best.

- After you've finished the test, review the answer key to see where you went wrong.

- Use the answer sheet provided to record your answers. (You can cut it out or photocopy it)

- You will receive 1 point for every correct answer, and you will lose $\frac{1}{4}$ point for each incorrect answer. There is no penalty for skipping a question.

Calculators are NOT permitted for the ISEE Upper Level Test

Good Luck!

ISEE Upper Level Math Practice Test 1

2019 - 2020

Two Parts

Total number of questions: 84

Part 1 (Calculator): 37 questions

Part 2 (Calculator): 47 questions

Total time for two parts: 75 Minutes

ISEE Upper Level Practice Test Answer Sheets

Remove (or photocopy) this answer sheet and use it to complete the practice test.

ISEE Upper Level Practice Test 1

Quantitative Reasoning		Mathematics Achievement	
1 (A) (B) (C) (D)	25 (A) (B) (C) (D)	1 (A) (B) (C) (D)	25 (A) (B) (C) (D)
2 (A) (B) (C) (D)	26 (A) (B) (C) (D)	2 (A) (B) (C) (D)	26 (A) (B) (C) (D)
3 (A) (B) (C) (D)	27 (A) (B) (C) (D)	3 (A) (B) (C) (D)	27 (A) (B) (C) (D)
4 (A) (B) (C) (D)	28 (A) (B) (C) (D)	4 (A) (B) (C) (D)	28 (A) (B) (C) (D)
5 (A) (B) (C) (D)	29 (A) (B) (C) (D)	5 (A) (B) (C) (D)	29 (A) (B) (C) (D)
6 (A) (B) (C) (D)	30 (A) (B) (C) (D)	6 (A) (B) (C) (D)	30 (A) (B) (C) (D)
7 (A) (B) (C) (D)	31 (A) (B) (C) (D)	7 (A) (B) (C) (D)	31 (A) (B) (C) (D)
8 (A) (B) (C) (D)	32 (A) (B) (C) (D)	8 (A) (B) (C) (D)	32 (A) (B) (C) (D)
9 (A) (B) (C) (D)	33 (A) (B) (C) (D)	9 (A) (B) (C) (D)	33 (A) (B) (C) (D)
10 (A) (B) (C) (D)	34 (A) (B) (C) (D)	10 (A) (B) (C) (D)	34 (A) (B) (C) (D)
11 (A) (B) (C) (D)	35 (A) (B) (C) (D)	11 (A) (B) (C) (D)	35 (A) (B) (C) (D)
12 (A) (B) (C) (D)	36 (A) (B) (C) (D)	12 (A) (B) (C) (D)	36 (A) (B) (C) (D)
13 (A) (B) (C) (D)	37 (A) (B) (C) (D)	13 (A) (B) (C) (D)	37 (A) (B) (C) (D)
14 (A) (B) (C) (D)		14 (A) (B) (C) (D)	38 (A) (B) (C) (D)
15 (A) (B) (C) (D)		15 (A) (B) (C) (D)	39 (A) (B) (C) (D)
16 (A) (B) (C) (D)		16 (A) (B) (C) (D)	40 (A) (B) (C) (D)
17 (A) (B) (C) (D)		17 (A) (B) (C) (D)	41 (A) (B) (C) (D)
18 (A) (B) (C) (D)		18 (A) (B) (C) (D)	42 (A) (B) (C) (D)
19 (A) (B) (C) (D)		19 (A) (B) (C) (D)	43 (A) (B) (C) (D)
20 (A) (B) (C) (D)		20 (A) (B) (C) (D)	44 (A) (B) (C) (D)
21 (A) (B) (C) (D)		21 (A) (B) (C) (D)	45 (A) (B) (C) (D)
22 (A) (B) (C) (D)		22 (A) (B) (C) (D)	46 (A) (B) (C) (D)
23 (A) (B) (C) (D)		23 (A) (B) (C) (D)	47 (A) (B) (C) (D)
24 (A) (B) (C) (D)		24 (A) (B) (C) (D)	

ISEE Upper Level Math Practice Test 1

Part 1 (Quantitative Reasoning)

- ○ **37 questions**
- ○ **Total time for this section:** 35 Minutes

You may NOT use a calculator for this test.

1) What is the area of a square whose diagonal is 4?
   A. 4
   B. 6
   C. 8
   D. 16

2) There are 6 blue marbles, 8 red marbles, and 5 yellow marbles in a box. If Ava randomly selects a marble from the box, what is the probability of selecting a red or yellow marble?
   A. $\frac{1}{6}$
   B. $\frac{1}{5}$
   C. $\frac{13}{19}$
   D. $\frac{5}{8}$

3) Which of the following is NOT a factor of 80?
   A. 8
   B. 10
   C. 14
   D. 16

4) If Emily left a $12.25 tip on a breakfast that cost $68.65, approximately what percentage was the tip?
   A. 18%
   B. 16%
   C. 14%
   D. 12%

5) A phone company charges $4 for the first six minutes of a phone call and 40 cents per minute thereafter. If Sofia makes a phone call that lasts 36 minutes, what will be the total cost of the phone call?
   A. 16.00
   B. 16.50
   C. 17.00
   D. 17.50

6) Michelle and Alec can finish a job together in 100 minutes. If Michelle can do the job by herself in 5 hours, how many minutes does it take Alec to finish the job?
   A. 120
   B. 150
   C. 180
   D. 200

7) James earns $7.50 per hour and worked 30 hours. Jacob earns $9.00 per hour. How many hours would Jacob need to work to equal James's earnings over 30 hours?
   A. 15
   B. 20
   C. 25
   D. 30

8) On a map, the length of the road from City A to City B is measured to be 20 inches. On this map, $\frac{1}{3}$ inch represents an actual distance of 12 miles. What is the actual distance, in miles, from City A to City B along this road?
   A. 580 miles
   B. 720 miles
   C. 960 miles
   D. 1,140 miles

A library has 840 books that include Mathematics, Physics, Chemistry, English and History.

Use following graph to answer questions 9 .

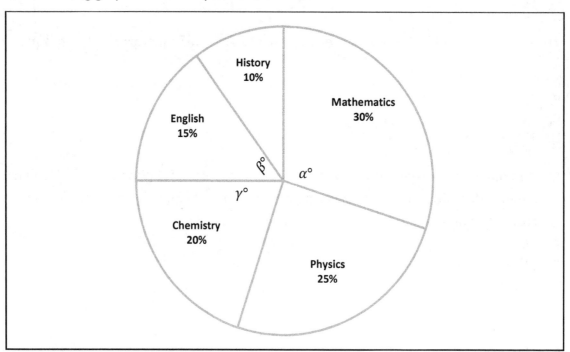

9) What is the product of the number of Mathematics and number of English books?
   A. 41,168
   B. 31,752
   C. 26,460
   D. 17,640

10) If 150% of a number is 75, then what is the 80% of that number?
A. 40
B. 50
C. 60
D. 70

11) If $3y + 5 < 29$, then y could be equal to?
A. 15
B. 12
C. 10.5
D. 2.5

12) In the figure, MN is 40 cm. How long is ON?
A. 25 cm
B. 20 cm
C. 15 cm
D. 10 cm

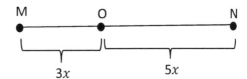

13) The first four terms in a sequence are shown below. What is the sixth term in the sequence?

$$\{2, 5, 10, 17, \dots\}$$

A. 37
B. 39
C. 41
D. 50

14) Emily and Daniel have taken the same number of photos on their school trip. Emily has taken 5 times as many as photos as Claire and Daniel has taken 16 more photos than Claire. How many photos has Claire taken?
A. 4
B. 6
C. 8
D. 10

15) What is the equation of the line that passes through $(2, -2)$ and has a slope of 7?
A. $y = 7x - 16$
B. $y = 7x - 12$
C. $y = 7x + 16$
D. $y = 7x + 12$

16) How many $\frac{1}{5}$ pound paperback books together weigh 50 pounds?

A. 25

B. 50

C. 150

D. 250

17) A supermarket's sales increased by 10 percent in the month of April and decreased by 10 percent in the month of May. What is the percent change in the sales of the supermarket over the two-month period?

A. 1% decrease

B. No change

C. 1% increase

D. 1.1% increase

18) Find the solution (x, y) to the following system of equations?
$$-3x - y = 6$$
$$6x + 4y = 10$$

A. $(14, 5)$

B. $(6, 8)$

C. $(11, 17)$

D. $(-\frac{17}{3}, 11)$

19) The distance between cities A and B is approximately 2,600 miles. If Alice drives an average of 68 miles per hour, how many hours will it take Alice to drive from city A to city B?

A. *Approximately* 41 *hours*

B. *Approximately* 38 *hours*

C. *Approximately* 29 *hours*

D. *Approximately* 27 *hours*

20) Two third of 18 is equal to $\frac{2}{5}$ of what number?

A. 12

B. 20

C. 30

D. 60

21) Sophia purchased a sofa for $530.40. The sofa is regularly priced at $624. What was the percent discount Sophia received on the sofa?

A. 12%

B. 15%

C. 20%

D. 25%

Quantitative Comparisons

Direction: Questions 22 to 37 are Quantitative Comparisons Questions. Using the information provided in each question, compare the quantity in column A to the quantity in Column B. Choose on your answer sheet grid

A   if the quantity in Column A is greater

B   if the quantity in Column B is greater

C   if the two quantities are equal

D   if the relationship cannot be determined from the information given

22)

Column A	Column B
5%	$\frac{1}{2}$

23) Set A includes even prime numbers.

Column A	Column B
The sum of all members in Set A	2

24)

Column A	Column B
The number of posts needed for a fence 100 feet long if the posts are placed 12.5 feet apart	8 posts

25)

Column A	Column B
The average of $12, 18, 26, 30, 32$	The average of $24, 28, 30, 36$

26)

Column A	Column B
$9 + 12(9 - 5)$	$12 + 9(9 - 5)$

27) $\dfrac{x}{48} = \dfrac{2}{3}$

Column A	Column B
$\dfrac{8}{x}$	$\dfrac{1}{4}$

28) Working at constant rates, machine D makes b rolls of steel in 25 minutes and machine E makes b rolls of steel in one hour ($b > 0$)

Column A	Column B
The number of rolls of steel made by machine D in 2 hours and 5 minutes.	The number of rolls of steel made by machine E in 4 hours.

29) The ratio of boys to girls in a class is 7 to 11.

Column A	Column B
Ratio of boys to the entire class	$\dfrac{1}{3}$

30) There are 6 blue marbles and 4 green marbles in a jar. Two marbles are pulled out in succession without replacing them in the jar.

Column A	Column B
The probability that both marbles are blue.	The probability that the first marbles is green, but the second is blue.

31) $\dfrac{x}{4} = y^2$

Column A	Column B
x	y

32) $x = -1$

Column A	Column B
$3x^2 - 2x + 4$	$2x^3 + x^2 + 4$

33) $6 > y > -2$

Column A	Column B
$\dfrac{y}{4}$	$\dfrac{4}{y}$

34) $\dfrac{a}{b} = \dfrac{c}{d}$

Column A	Column B

$$a + b \qquad\qquad\qquad c + d$$

35) A magazine printer consecutively numbered the pages of a magazine, starting with 1 on the first page, 10 on the tenth page, etc. In numbering the gages, the printer printed a total of 195 digits.

Column A	Column B
The number of pages in the magazine	100

36)

Column A	Column B
The largest number that can be written by rearranging the digits in 263	The largest number that can be written by rearranging the digits in 192

37) A computer priced $124 includes 4% profit

Column A	Column B
$119	The original cost of the computer

IF YOU FINISH BEFORE TIME IS CALLED, YOU MAY CHECK YOUR WORK ON THIS SECTION ONLY. DO NOT TURN TO ANY OTHER SECTION IN THE TEST. STOP

ISEE Upper Level Math
Practice Test 1

Part 2 (Mathematics Achievement)

- **47 questions**
- **Total time for this section:** 40 Minutes

You may NOT use a calculator for this test.

1) Find all values of x for which $4x^2 + 14x + 6 = 0$

A. $-\dfrac{3}{2}, -\dfrac{1}{2}$

B. $-\dfrac{1}{2}, -3$

C. $-2, -\dfrac{1}{3}$

D. $-\dfrac{2}{3}, \dfrac{1}{2}$

2) $(x + 7)(x + 5) =$

A. $x^2 + 12x + 12$

B. $2x + 12x + 12$

C. $x^2 + 35x + 12$

D. $x^2 + 12x + 35$

3) Which of the following graphs represents the compound inequality $-4 \le 4x - 8 < 16$?

A.

B.

C.

D.

4) $|9 - (12 \div |2 - 5|)| = ?$

A. 9

B. -6

C. 5

D. -5

5) How is this number written in scientific notation?

$$0.00002389$$

A. 2.389×10^{-5}

B. 23.89×10^{6}

C. 0.2389×10^{-4}

D. 2389×10^{-8}

6) Which graph shows a non-proportional linear relationship between x and y?

A.

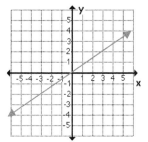

B.

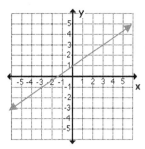

C.

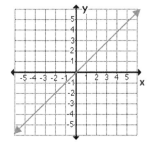

D.

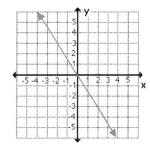

7) The rectangle on the coordinate grid is translated 5 units down and 4 units to the left.

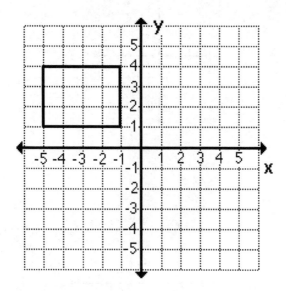

Which of the following describes this transformation?

A. $(x, y) \Rightarrow (x - 4, y + 5)$
B. $(x, y) \Rightarrow (x - 4, y - 5)$
C. $(x, y) \Rightarrow (x + 4, y + 5)$
D. $(x, y) \Rightarrow (x + 4, y - 5)$

8) A girl $160 \ cm$ tall, stands $360 \ cm$ from a lamp post at night. Her shadow from the light is $90 \ cm$ long. How high is the lamp post?
A. $240 \ cm$
B. $400 \ cm$
C. $600 \ cm$
D. $800 \ cm$

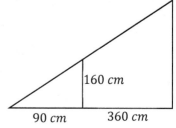

9) Which value of x makes the following inequality true?

$$\frac{3}{22} \le x < 19\%$$

A. 0.13
B. $\dfrac{5}{36}$
C. $\sqrt{0.044}$
D. 0.124

10) The ratio of boys to girls in a school is $2:3$. If there are 600 students in a school, how many boys are in the school?
A. 240
B. 360
C. 400
D. 540

11) $2 - 10 \div (4^2 \div 2) =$ ___
A. 6
B. $\frac{3}{4}$
C. -1
D. -2

12) When an integer is multiplied by itself, it can end in all of the following digits EXCEPT
A. 1
B. 6
C. 8
D. 9

13) Emily lives $5\frac{1}{4}$ miles from where she works. When traveling to work, she walks to a bus stop $\frac{1}{3}$ of the way to catch a bus. How many miles away from her house is the bus stop?

A. $4\frac{1}{3}$ Miles

B. $4\frac{3}{4}$ Miles

C. $2\frac{3}{4}$ Miles

D. $1\frac{3}{4}$ Miles

14) Use the diagram below to answer the question.

Given the lengths of the base and diagonal of the rectangle below, what is the length of height h, in terms of s?

A. $2s\sqrt{6}$
B. $s\sqrt{7}$
C. $5s$
D. $5s^2$

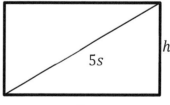

Use the chart below to answer the question.

Color	Number
White	20
Black	30
Beige	40

15) There are also purple marbles in the bag. Which of the following can NOT be the probability of randomly selecting a purple marble from the bag?

A. $\dfrac{1}{10}$

B. $\dfrac{1}{4}$

C. $\dfrac{2}{5}$

D. $\dfrac{7}{15}$

16) If the area of trapezoid is $126\ cm^2$, what is the perimeter of the trapezoid?

A. $12\ cm$
B. $32\ cm$
C. $46\ cm$
D. $55\ cm$

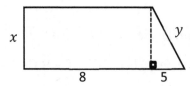

17) If a vehicle is driven 32 miles on Monday, 35 miles on Tuesday, and 29 miles on Wednesday, what is the average number of miles driven each day?
A. $32\ Miles$
B. $31\ Miles$
C. $29\ Miles$
D. $33\ Miles$

18) Find the area of a rectangle with a length of 138 feet and a width of 83 feet.
A. $11,504\ sq.ft$
B. $11,454\ sq.ft$
C. $11,404\ sq.ft$
D. $11,204\ sq.ft$

19) $89 \div \dfrac{1}{8} = ?$
A. 11.125
B. 12
C. 71
D. 712

20) With an 22% discount, Ella was able to save $20.42 on a dress. What was the original price of the dress?

A. $88.92
B. $90.82
C. $92.82
D. $93.92

21) $\frac{7}{25}$ is equals to:

A. 0.3
B. 2.8
C. 0.03
D. 0.28

22) If 20% of A is 1,600, what is 15% of A?

A. 800
B. 1,200
C. 1,600
D. 2,000

23) If $(5.2 + 9.3 + 1.5) \times x = x$, then what is the value of x?

A. 0
B. $\frac{3}{10}$
C. -4
D. -10

24) Two dice are thrown simultaneously, what is the probability of getting a sum of 6 or 9?

A. $\frac{1}{3}$
B. $\frac{1}{4}$
C. $\frac{1}{6}$
D. $\frac{1}{12}$

25) Simplify $\dfrac{\frac{1}{2} - \frac{x+5}{4}}{\frac{x^2}{2} - \frac{5}{2}}$

A. $\dfrac{3 - x}{x^2 - 10}$
B. $\dfrac{3 - x}{2x^2 - 10}$
C. $\dfrac{3 + x}{x^2 - 10}$
D. $\dfrac{-3 - x}{2x^2 - 10}$

26) In the following figure, AB is the diameter of the circle. What is the circumference of the circle?
   A. 5π
   B. 10π
   C. 15π
   D. 20π

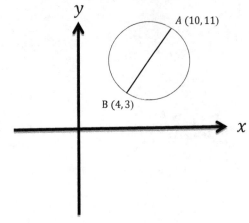

27) What is the value of x in the following equation?
$$2x^2 + 5 = 23$$
   A. ± 4
   B. ± 9
   C. ± 10
   D. ± 3

28) A circle has a diameter of 16 inches. What is its approximate area?
   A. $200.96\ sq.inch$
   B. $100.48\ sq.inch$
   C. $64.00\ sq.inch$
   D. $12.56\ sq.inch$

29) If 6 garbage trucks can collect the trash of 36 homes in a day. How many trucks are needed to collect in 180 houses?
   A. 18
   B. 19
   C. 15
   D. 30

30) $56.78 \div 0.06 = ?$
   A. 94.633
   B. 946.33
   C. 9463.3
   D. 9.4633

Use the following table to answer question below.

DANIEL'S BIRD-WATCHING PROJECT	
DAY	NUMBER OF RAPTORS SEEN
Monday	?
Tuesday	9
Wednesday	14
Thursday	12
Friday	5
MEAN	10

31) The above table shows the data Daniel collects while watching birds for one week. How many raptors did Daniel see on Monday?
A. 10
B. 11
C. 12
D. 13

32) A floppy disk shows 937,036 bytes free and 739,352 bytes used. If you delete a file of size 652,159 bytes and create a new file of size 599,986 bytes, how many free bytes will the floppy disk have?
A. 687,179 bytes
B. 791,525 bytes
C. 884,867 bytes
D. 989,209 bytes

33) $5\ days\ 19\ hours\ 35\ minutes - 3\ days\ 12\ hours\ 22\ minutes\ = ?$
A. $3\ days\ 10\ hours\ 13\ minutes$
B. $2\ days\ 7\ hours\ 13\ minutes$
C. $3\ days\ 10\ hours\ 13\ minutes$
D. $2\ days\ 7\ hours\ 23\ minutes$

34) The base of a right triangle is 2 feet, and the interior angles are $45 - 45 - 90$. What is its area?
A. $2\ square\ feet$
B. $4\ square\ feet$
C. $3.5\ square\ feet$
D. $5.5\ square\ feet$

35) Increased by 50%, the number 84 becomes:

A. 42
B. 100
C. 126
D. 130

36) Which equation represents the statement "twice the difference between 6 times H and 3 gives 30".

A. $\frac{6H + 3}{2} = 30$
B. $6(2H + 3) = 30$
C. $2(6H - 3) = 30$
D. $3\frac{6H}{2} = 30$

37) A circle is inscribed in a square, as shown below.

The area of the circle is $16\pi\ cm^2$. What is the area of the square?

A. $8cm^2$
B. $16\ cm^2$
C. $48\ cm^2$
D. $64cm^2$

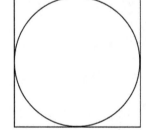

38) If $10 + x^{\frac{1}{2}} = 14$, then what is the value of $15 \times x$?

A. 15
B. 60
C. 120
D. 240

39) Triangle ABC is graphed on a coordinate grid with vertices at $A(-3,-2)$, $B(-1,4)$ and $C(7,9)$. Triangle ABC is reflected over x axes to create triangle $A'B'C'$.

Which order pair represents the coordinate of C'?

A. $(7,9)$
B. $(-7,-9)$
C. $(-7,9)$
D. $(7,-9)$

40) Which set of ordered pairs represents y as a function of x?
A. $\{(3,-2),(3,7),(9,-8),(4,-7)\}$
B. $\{(4,2),(3,-9),(5,8),(4,7)\}$
C. $\{(9,12),(5,7),(6,11),(5,18)\}$
D. $\{(6,1),(3,1),(0,5),(4,5)\}$

41) The width of a box is one third of its length. The height of the box is one third of its width. If the length of the box is 27 cm, what is the volume of the box?
A. 81 cm^3
B. 162 cm^3
C. 243 cm^3
D. 729cm^3

42) A square measures 6 inches on one side. By how much will the area be decreased if its length is increased by 5 inches and its width decreased by 3 inches.
A. 1 $sq\ decreased$
B. 3 $sq\ decreased$
C. 6 $sq\ decreased$
D. 9 $sq\ decreased$

43) If a box contains red and blue balls in ratio of 2 : 3 red to blue, how many red balls are there if 90 blue balls are in the box?
A. 40
B. 60
C. 80
D. 30

44) How many 3 × 3 squares can fit inside a rectangle with a height of 54 and width of 12?
A. 72
B. 62
C. 52
D. 42

45) David makes a weekly salary of $220 plus 8% commission on his sales. What will his income be for a week in which he makes sales totaling $1,100?
A. $328
B. $318
C. $308
D. $298

46) $4x^2y^3 + 5x^3y^5 - (5x^2y^3 - 2x^3y^5) =$ ___
A. $-x^2y^3$
B. $6x^2y^3 - x^3y^5$
C. $7x^2y^3$
D. $7x^3y^5 - x^2y^3$

47) The radius of circle A is three times the radius of circle B. If the circumference of circle A is 18π, what is the area of circle B?

A. 3π
B. 6π
C. 9π
D. 12π

IF YOU FINISH BEFORE TIME IS CALLED, YOU MAY CHECK YOUR WORK ON THIS SECTION.

STOP

ISEE Upper Level Math Practice Test 2

2019 - 2020

Two Parts

Total number of questions: 84

Part 1 (Calculator): 37 questions

Part 2 (Calculator): 47 questions

Total time for two parts: 75 Minutes

ISEE Upper Level Practice Test Answer Sheets

Remove (or photocopy) this answer sheet and use it to complete the practice test.

ISEE Upper Level Practice Test 2

Quantitative Reasoning Mathematics Achievement

1	Ⓐ Ⓑ Ⓒ Ⓓ	25	Ⓐ Ⓑ Ⓒ Ⓓ	1	Ⓐ Ⓑ Ⓒ Ⓓ	25	Ⓐ Ⓑ Ⓒ Ⓓ
2	Ⓐ Ⓑ Ⓒ Ⓓ	26	Ⓐ Ⓑ Ⓒ Ⓓ	2	Ⓐ Ⓑ Ⓒ Ⓓ	26	Ⓐ Ⓑ Ⓒ Ⓓ
3	Ⓐ Ⓑ Ⓒ Ⓓ	27	Ⓐ Ⓑ Ⓒ Ⓓ	3	Ⓐ Ⓑ Ⓒ Ⓓ	27	Ⓐ Ⓑ Ⓒ Ⓓ
4	Ⓐ Ⓑ Ⓒ Ⓓ	28	Ⓐ Ⓑ Ⓒ Ⓓ	4	Ⓐ Ⓑ Ⓒ Ⓓ	28	Ⓐ Ⓑ Ⓒ Ⓓ
5	Ⓐ Ⓑ Ⓒ Ⓓ	29	Ⓐ Ⓑ Ⓒ Ⓓ	5	Ⓐ Ⓑ Ⓒ Ⓓ	29	Ⓐ Ⓑ Ⓒ Ⓓ
6	Ⓐ Ⓑ Ⓒ Ⓓ	30	Ⓐ Ⓑ Ⓒ Ⓓ	6	Ⓐ Ⓑ Ⓒ Ⓓ	30	Ⓐ Ⓑ Ⓒ Ⓓ
7	Ⓐ Ⓑ Ⓒ Ⓓ	31	Ⓐ Ⓑ Ⓒ Ⓓ	7	Ⓐ Ⓑ Ⓒ Ⓓ	31	Ⓐ Ⓑ Ⓒ Ⓓ
8	Ⓐ Ⓑ Ⓒ Ⓓ	32	Ⓐ Ⓑ Ⓒ Ⓓ	8	Ⓐ Ⓑ Ⓒ Ⓓ	32	Ⓐ Ⓑ Ⓒ Ⓓ
9	Ⓐ Ⓑ Ⓒ Ⓓ	33	Ⓐ Ⓑ Ⓒ Ⓓ	9	Ⓐ Ⓑ Ⓒ Ⓓ	33	Ⓐ Ⓑ Ⓒ Ⓓ
10	Ⓐ Ⓑ Ⓒ Ⓓ	34	Ⓐ Ⓑ Ⓒ Ⓓ	10	Ⓐ Ⓑ Ⓒ Ⓓ	34	Ⓐ Ⓑ Ⓒ Ⓓ
11	Ⓐ Ⓑ Ⓒ Ⓓ	35	Ⓐ Ⓑ Ⓒ Ⓓ	11	Ⓐ Ⓑ Ⓒ Ⓓ	35	Ⓐ Ⓑ Ⓒ Ⓓ
12	Ⓐ Ⓑ Ⓒ Ⓓ	36	Ⓐ Ⓑ Ⓒ Ⓓ	12	Ⓐ Ⓑ Ⓒ Ⓓ	36	Ⓐ Ⓑ Ⓒ Ⓓ
13	Ⓐ Ⓑ Ⓒ Ⓓ	37	Ⓐ Ⓑ Ⓒ Ⓓ	13	Ⓐ Ⓑ Ⓒ Ⓓ	37	Ⓐ Ⓑ Ⓒ Ⓓ
14	Ⓐ Ⓑ Ⓒ Ⓓ			14	Ⓐ Ⓑ Ⓒ Ⓓ	38	Ⓐ Ⓑ Ⓒ Ⓓ
15	Ⓐ Ⓑ Ⓒ Ⓓ			15	Ⓐ Ⓑ Ⓒ Ⓓ	39	Ⓐ Ⓑ Ⓒ Ⓓ
16	Ⓐ Ⓑ Ⓒ Ⓓ			16	Ⓐ Ⓑ Ⓒ Ⓓ	40	Ⓐ Ⓑ Ⓒ Ⓓ
17	Ⓐ Ⓑ Ⓒ Ⓓ			17	Ⓐ Ⓑ Ⓒ Ⓓ	41	Ⓐ Ⓑ Ⓒ Ⓓ
18	Ⓐ Ⓑ Ⓒ Ⓓ			18	Ⓐ Ⓑ Ⓒ Ⓓ	42	Ⓐ Ⓑ Ⓒ Ⓓ
19	Ⓐ Ⓑ Ⓒ Ⓓ			19	Ⓐ Ⓑ Ⓒ Ⓓ	43	Ⓐ Ⓑ Ⓒ Ⓓ
20	Ⓐ Ⓑ Ⓒ Ⓓ			20	Ⓐ Ⓑ Ⓒ Ⓓ	44	Ⓐ Ⓑ Ⓒ Ⓓ
21	Ⓐ Ⓑ Ⓒ Ⓓ			21	Ⓐ Ⓑ Ⓒ Ⓓ	45	Ⓐ Ⓑ Ⓒ Ⓓ
22	Ⓐ Ⓑ Ⓒ Ⓓ			22	Ⓐ Ⓑ Ⓒ Ⓓ	46	Ⓐ Ⓑ Ⓒ Ⓓ
23	Ⓐ Ⓑ Ⓒ Ⓓ			23	Ⓐ Ⓑ Ⓒ Ⓓ	47	Ⓐ Ⓑ Ⓒ Ⓓ
24	Ⓐ Ⓑ Ⓒ Ⓓ			24	Ⓐ Ⓑ Ⓒ Ⓓ		

ISEE Upper Level

Practice Test 2

Part 1 (Quantitative Reasoning)

- ○ **37 questions**
- ○ **Total time for this section:** 35 Minutes
- ○ **Calculators are not allowed at the test.**

1) What is the prime factorization of 560?
A. $2 \times 2 \times 5 \times 7$
B. $2 \times 2 \times 2 \times 2 \times 5 \times 7$
C. 2×7
D. $2 \times 2 \times 2 \times 5 \times 7$

2) A basket contains 20 balls and the average weight of each of these balls is 25 g. The five heaviest balls have an average weight of 40 g each. If we remove the three heaviest balls from the basket, what is the average weight of the remaining balls?
A. 10 g
B. 20 g
C. 30 g
D. 35 g

3) How much greater is the value of $5x + 8$ than the value of $5x - 3$?
A. 7
B. 9
C. 11
D. 13

4) If 5 inches on a map represents an actual distance of 100 feet, then what actual distance does 18 inches on the map represent?
A. 18 feet
B. 100 feet
C. 250 feet
D. 360 feet

5) The circle graph below shows all Mr. Green's expenses for last month. If he spent $660 on his car, how much did he spend for his rent?

A. $700
B. $740
C. $780
D. $810

Mr. Green's monthly expenses

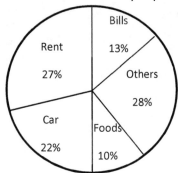

6) Alice drives from her house to work at an average speed of 55 miles per hour and she drives at an average speed of 62 miles per hour when she was returning home. What was her minimum speed on the round trip in miles per hour?

A. 55
B. 58.5
C. 62
D. Cannot be determined

7) The area of a circle is less than $64\,\pi$. Which of the following can be the circumference of the circle?

A. $12\,\pi$
B. $16\,\pi$
C. $24\,\pi$
D. $32\,\pi$

8) Oscar purchased a new hat that was on sale for $7.35. The original price was $12.65. What percentage discount was the sale price?

A. 4.2%
B. 40.5%
C. 42%
D. 45%

9) If $f(x) = x^2 + 5$, what is the smallest possible value of $f(x)$?

A. 0
B. 4
C. 5
D. 7

10) If the sum of the positive integers from 1 to n is 2,250, and the sum of the positive integers from $n + 1$ to $2n$ is 4,356, which of the following represents the sum of the positive integers from 1 to $2n$ inclusive?

A. 2,106
B. 4,356
C. 6,000
D. 6,606

11) Which of the following statements is correct, according to the graph below?

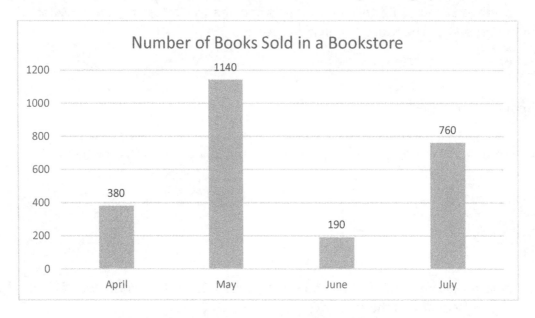

A. Number of books sold in April was twice the number of books sold in July.
B. Number of books sold in July was less than half the number of books sold in May.
C. Number of books sold in June was half the number of books sold in April.
D. Number of books sold in July was equal to the number of books sold in April plus the number of books sold in June.

12) List A consists of the numbers $\{1, 3, 8, 10, 15\}$, and list B consists of the numbers $\{4, 6, 12, 14, 17\}$.

   If the two lists are combined, what is the median of the combined list?

A. 6
B. 8
C. 9
D. 10

13) If Jim adds 100 stamps to his current stamp collection, the total number of stamps will be equal to $\frac{6}{5}$ the current number of stamps. If Jim adds 50% more stamps to the current collection, how many stamps will be in the collection?

A. 150
B. 300
C. 600
D. 750

14) A bag contains 18 balls: two green, five black, eight blue, a brown, a red and one white. If 17 balls are removed from the bag at random, what is the probability that a brown ball has been removed?

A. $\frac{1}{9}$

B. $\frac{1}{6}$

C. $\frac{16}{17}$

D. $\frac{17}{18}$

15) If $x + y = 8$ and $x - y = 5$ then what is the value of $(x^2 - y^2)$?

A. 23

B. 40

C. 65

D. 90

16) What's The ratio of boys and girls in a class is $4:7$. If there are 44 students in the class, how many more boys should be enrolled to make the ratio $1:1$?

A. 8

B. 10

C. 12

D. 16

17) The area of rectangle $ABCD$ is 196 square inches. If the length of the rectangle is four times the width, what is the perimeter of rectangle $ABCD$?

A. 56 inches

B. 70 inches

C. 84 inches

D. 90 inches

18) The sum of 8 numbers is greater than 160 and less than 240. Which of the following could be the average (arithmetic mean) of the numbers?

A. 20

B. 25

C. 40

D. 45

19) Which of the following expressions gives the value of b in terms of a, c, and z from the following equation?

$$a = [\frac{cz}{b}]^2$$

A. $b = ac^2z^2$

B. $b = \frac{cz}{\sqrt{a}}$

C. $b = \frac{\sqrt{a}}{cz}$

D. $b = [\frac{cz}{a}]^2$

20) Triangle ABC is similar to triangle ADE. What is the length of side EC?

A. 4

B. 9

C. 18

D. 45

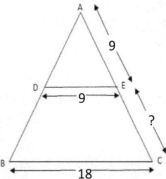

21) A gas tank can hold 25 gallons when it is $\frac{2}{5}$ full. How many gallons does it contain when it is full?

A. 125

B. 62.5

C. 50

D. 10

Quantitative Comparisons

Direction: Questions 22 to 37 are Quantitative Comparisons Questions. Using the information provided in each question, compare the quantity in column A to the quantity in Column B. Choose on your answer sheet grid

    A   if the quantity in Column A is greater
    B   if the quantity in Column B is greater
    C   if the two quantities are equal
    D   if the relationship cannot be determined from the information given

22)

Column A	Column B
The average of $15, 25,$ and 27	20

23)

Column A	Column B
$11 \times 675 \times 24$	$18 \times 675 \times 17$

24) x is an integer

Column A	Column B
x	$\dfrac{x}{-2}$

25)

Column A	Column B
The greatest value of x in	The greatest value of x in
$6\,|2x - 4| = 6$	$6\,|2x + 4| = 6$

26) x is an integer

Column A	Column B
$(x)^3(x)^4$	$(x^3)^4$

27)

Column A	Column B
The probability that	The probability that
event x will occur.	event x will not occur.

28)

Column A	Column B
2^2	$\sqrt[3]{64}$

29)

Column A	Column B
8	$(59)^{\frac{1}{2}}$

30) The selling price of a sport jacket including 25% discount is \$51.

Column A	Column B
Original price of the sport jacket	\$67

31)

Column A	Column B
$(0.69)^{34}$	$(0.69)^{33}$

32)

Column A	Column B
The probability of rolling a 6 on a die and getting heads on a coin toss.	The probability of rolling an even number on a die and picking a spade from a deck of 52 cards.

33)

Column A	Column B
$(\frac{1}{5})^2$	5^{-2}

34) $x + 2 > 5x$

Column A	Column B
x	-1

35)

Column A	Column B
$0.41	Sum of one quarter, two nickels, and three pennies

36) x is an odd integer, and y is an even integer. In a certain game an odd number is considered greater than an even number.

Column A	Column B
$(x + y)^2 - y$	$(y)(x - y)$

37) $x^2 - 5x - 8 = 6$

Column A	Column B
x	0

IF YOU FINISH BEFORE TIME IS CALLED, YOU MAY CHECK YOUR WORK ON THIS SECTION ONLY. DO NOT TURN TO ANY OTHER SECTION IN THE TEST. **STOP**

ISEE Upper Level

Practice Test 2

Part 2 (Mathematics Achievement)

- o **47 questions**
- o **Total time for this section:** 40 Minutes
- o **Calculators are not allowed at the test.**

1) $\dfrac{1}{6b^2} + \dfrac{1}{6b} = \dfrac{1}{b^2}$, then b = ?

A. $-\dfrac{16}{15}$

B. 5

C. $-\dfrac{15}{16}$

D. 8

2) If $\dfrac{|3+x|}{7} \leq 5$, then which of the following is correct?

A. $-38 \leq x \leq 35$

B. $-38 \leq x \leq 32$

C. $-32 \leq x \leq 38$

D. $-32 \leq x \leq 32$

3) The cost, in thousands of dollars, of producing x thousands of textbooks is $C(x) = x^2 + 2x$. The revenue, also in thousands of dollars, is $R(x) = 40x$. find the profit or loss if 30 textbooks are produced. ($profit = revenue - cost$)

A. $2,160 $profit$

B. $240 $profit$

C. $2,160 $loss$

D. $240 $loss$

4) Ella (E) is 4 years older than her friend Ava (A) who is 3 years younger than her sister Sofia (S). If E, A and S denote their ages, which one of the following represents the given information?

A. $\begin{cases} E = A + 4 \\ S = A - 3 \end{cases}$

B. $\begin{cases} E = A + 4 \\ A = S + 3 \end{cases}$

C. $\begin{cases} A = E + 4 \\ S = A - 3 \end{cases}$

D. $\begin{cases} E = A + 4 \\ A = S - 3 \end{cases}$

5) 5 less than twice a positive integer is 83. What is the integer?

A. 39

B. 41

C. 42

D. 44

6) Which of the following points lies on the line $4x + 6y = 14$?
A. $(2, 1)$
B. $(-1, 2)$
C. $(-2, 2)$
D. $(2, 2)$

7) An angle is equal to one fifth of its supplement. What is the measure of that angle?
A. $20°$
B. $30°$
C. $45°$
D. $60°$

8) 1.2 is what percent of 24?
A. 1.2
B. 5
C. 12
D. 24

9) Right triangle ABC has two legs of lengths $6\ cm$ (AB) and $8\ cm$ (AC). What is the length of the third side (BC)?
A. $4\ cm$
B. $6\ cm$
C. $8\ cm$
D. $10\ cm$

10) Simplify $6x^2y^3(2x^2y)^3 =$
A. $12x^4y^6$
B. $12x^8y^6$
C. $48x^4y^6$
D. $48x^8y^6$

11) Which is the longest time?
A. $23\ hours$
B. $1520\ minutes$
C. $2\ days$
D. $4200\ seconds$

12) Write 523 in expanded form, using exponents.
A. $(5 \times 10^3) + (2 \times 10^2) + (3 \times 10)$
B. $(5 \times 10^2) + (2 \times 10^1) - 5$
C. $(5 \times 10^2) + (2 \times 10^1) + 3$
D. $(5 \times 10^1) + (2 \times 10^2) + 3$

13) A company pays its writer $4 for every 400 words written. How much will a writer earn for an article with 960 words?

A. $11
B. $5.6
C. $9.6
D. $10.7

14) A circular logo is enlarged to fit the lid of a jar. The new diameter is 30% larger than the original. By what percentage has the area of the logo increased?

A. 20%
B. 30%
C. 69%
D. 75%

15) A circle has a diameter of 8 inches. What is its approximate circumference?

A. 6.28 inches
B. 25.12 inches
C. 34.85 inches
D. 35.12 inches

16) What is the area of an isosceles right triangle with hypotenuse that measures $6\ cm$?

A. $9\ cm^2$
B. $18\ cm^2$
C. $3\ \sqrt{2}\ cm^2$
D. $36\ cm^2$

17) What's the area of the non-shaded part of the following figure?

A. 192
B. 152
C. 40
D. 42

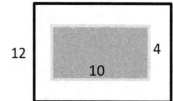

12   4

10

16

18) $79.22 \div 0.05 = ?$

A. 15.844
B. 1,584.4
C. 158.44
D. 1.5844

19) A bread recipe calls for $3\frac{1}{3}$ cups of flour. If you only have $2\frac{5}{6}$ cups, how much more flour is needed?

A. 1

B. $\frac{1}{2}$

C. 2

D. $\frac{5}{6}$

20) The equation of a line is given as: $y = 5x - 3$. Which of the following points does not lie on the line?

A. $(1, 2)$

B. $(-2, -13)$

C. $(3, 18)$

D. $(2, 7)$

21) The drivers at $G \& G$ trucking must report the mileage on their trucks each week. The mileage reading of Ed's vehicle was 40,907 at the beginning of one week, and 41,053 at the end of the same week. What was the total number of miles driven by Ed that week?

A. 46 *MILES*

B. 145 *MILES*

C. 146 *MILES*

D. 1,046 *MILES*

22) What is the maximum value for y if $y = -(x-2)^2 + 6$?

A. -6

B. -2

C. 2

D. 6

23) What is the solution of the following system of equations?

$$\begin{cases} -2x - y = -9 \\ 5x - 2y = 18 \end{cases}$$

A. $(-1, 2)$

B. $(4, 1)$

C. $(1, 4)$

D. $(4, -2)$

24) What is the area of an isosceles right triangle that has one leg that measures $6\ cm$?
A. $18\ cm^2$
B. $36\ cm^2$
C. $6\sqrt{2}\ cm^2$
D. $72\ cm^2$

25) Which of the following is a factor of both $x^2 - 2x - 8$ and $x^2 - 6x + 8$?

A. $(x - 4)$
B. $(x + 4)$
C. $(x - 2)$
D. $(x + 2)$

26) $\dfrac{13}{25}$ is equal to:
A. 5.2
B. 0.52
C. 0.05
D. 0.5

27) If $x + y = 12$, what is the value of $8x + 8y$?
A. 192
B. 104
C. 96
D. 48

28)
$$\begin{array}{r} 37\ hr.\ 25\ min. \\ -\ 24\ hr.\ 38\ min. \\ \hline \end{array}$$
A. $12\ hr.\ 57\ min.$
B. $12\ hr.\ 47\ min.$
C. $13\ hr.\ 13\ min.$
D. $13\ hr.\ 57\ min.$

29) A car uses 15 gallons of gas to travel 450 miles. How many miles per gallon does the car use?
A. $28\ miles\ per\ gallon$
B. $32\ miles\ per\ gallon$
C. $30\ miles\ per\ gallon$
D. $34\ miles\ per\ gallon$

30) What is the number of cubic feet of soil needed for a flower box 2 feet long, 8 inches wide, and 2 feet deep?
   A. $32\ cubic\ feet$
   B. $16\ cubic\ feet$
   C. $\frac{8}{3}\ cubic\ feet$
   D. $2\ cubic\ feet$

31) What is the reciprocal of $\frac{x^3}{16}$?
   A. $\frac{16}{x^3} - 1$
   B. $\frac{48}{x^3}$
   C. $\frac{16}{x^3} + 1$
   D. $\frac{16}{x^3}$

32) Mario loaned Jett $1,200 at a yearly interest rate of 5%. After one year what is the interest owned on this loan?
   A. $1,260
   B. $120
   C. $60
   D. $30

33) Ellis just got hired for on-the-road sales and will travel about 2,500 miles a week during an 80-hour work week. If the time spent traveling is $\frac{3}{5}$ of his week, how many hours a week will he be on the road?
   A. Ellis spends about 34 hours of his 80-hour work week on the road.
   B. Ellis spends about 40 hours of his 80-hour work week on the road.
   C. Ellis spends about 43 hours of his 80-hour work week on the road.
   D. Ellis spends about 48 hours of his 80-hour work week on the road.

34) Given that $x = 0.6$ and $y = 6$, what is the value of $2x^2(y + 4)$?
   A. 7.2
   B. 8.2
   C. 11.2
   D. 13.2

35) Karen is 9 years older than her sister Michelle, and Michelle is 4 years younger than her brother David. If the sum of their ages is 82, how old is Michelle?
   A. 21
   B. 23
   C. 25
   D. 29

36) Calculate the area of a parallelogram with a base of 2 feet and height of 2.4 feet.
   A. 2.8 *square feet*
   B. 4.2 *square feet*
   C. 4.8 *square feet*
   D. 8 *square feet*

37) A shirt costing $200 is discounted 25%. After a month, the shirt is discounted another 15%. Which of the following expressions can be used to find the selling price of the shirt?
   A. $(200)\,(0.70)$
   B. $(200) - 200\,(0.30)$
   C. $(200)(0.15) - (200)\,(0.15)$
   D. $(200)\,(0.75)\,(0.85)$

38) In a school, the ratio of number of boys to girls is $3:7$. If the number of boys is 180, what is the total number of students in the school?
   A. 390
   B. 500
   C. 540
   D. 600

39) A tree 32 feet tall casts a shadow 12 feet long. Jack is 6 feet tall. How long is Jack's shadow?
   A. 2.25 *ft*
   B. 4 *ft*
   C. 4.25 *ft*
   D. 8 *ft*

40) What is the area of the shaded region if the diameter of the bigger circle is 12 *inches* and the diameter of the smaller circle is 8 inches.

A. $16\,\pi\ inch^2$
B. $20\,\pi\ inch^2$
C. $36\,\pi\ inch^2$
D. $80\,\pi\ inch^2$

41) What is the result of the expression?

$$\begin{vmatrix} 3 & 6 \\ -1 & -3 \\ -5 & -1 \end{vmatrix} + \begin{vmatrix} 0 & -1 \\ 6 & 0 \\ 2 & 3 \end{vmatrix}$$

A. $\begin{vmatrix} 0 & -1 \\ 6 & 0 \\ 2 & 3 \end{vmatrix}$

B. $\begin{vmatrix} 3 & 6 \\ -1 & -3 \\ -5 & -1 \end{vmatrix}$

C. $\begin{vmatrix} 3 & 5 \\ 5 & -3 \\ -3 & 2 \end{vmatrix}$

D. $\begin{vmatrix} 0 & -3 \\ -6 & 0 \\ -10 & -3 \end{vmatrix}$

42) How many square feet of tile is needed for a 18 feet × 18 feet room?
   A. $72\ square\ feet$
   B. $108\ square\ feet$
   C. $324\ square\ feet$
   D. $416\ square\ feet$

43) $(3x + 3)(x + 5) =$
   A. $4x + 8$
   B. $3x + 3x + 15$
   C. $3x^2 + 18x + 15$
   D. $3x^2 + 3$

44) If $x\blacksquare y = \sqrt{x^2 + y}$, what is the value of $5\blacksquare11$?

   A. $\sqrt{126}$
   B. 6
   C. 4
   D. 3

45) There are three equal tanks of water. If $\frac{2}{5}$ of a tank contains 200 liters of water, what is the capacity of the three tanks of water together?
   A. 1,500 liters
   B. 500 liters
   C. 240 liters
   D. 80 liters

46) The average weight of 18 girls in a class is $60 \, kg$ and the average weight of 32 boys in the same class is $62 \, kg$. What is the average weight of all the 50 students in that class?
A. $60 \, kg$
B. $61.28 \, kg$
C. $61.68 \, kg$
D. $61.9 \, kg$

47) If x is 45% percent of 820, what is x?
A. 185
B. 369
C. 402
D. 720

IF YOU FINISH BEFORE TIME IS CALLED, YOU MAY CHECK YOUR WORK ON THIS SECTION.

STOP

ISEE Upper Level Math Practice Test 3

2019 - 2020

Two Parts

Total number of questions: 84

Part 1 (Calculator): 37 questions

Part 2 (Calculator): 47 questions

Total time for two parts: 75 Minutes

ISEE Upper Level Practice Test Answer Sheets

Remove (or photocopy) this answer sheet and use it to complete the practice test.

	ISEE Upper Level Practice Test 3	
Quantitative Reasoning		**Mathematics Achievement**

Quantitative Reasoning

1. Ⓐ Ⓑ Ⓒ Ⓓ   25. Ⓐ Ⓑ Ⓒ Ⓓ
2. Ⓐ Ⓑ Ⓒ Ⓓ   26. Ⓐ Ⓑ Ⓒ Ⓓ
3. Ⓐ Ⓑ Ⓒ Ⓓ   27. Ⓐ Ⓑ Ⓒ Ⓓ
4. Ⓐ Ⓑ Ⓒ Ⓓ   28. Ⓐ Ⓑ Ⓒ Ⓓ
5. Ⓐ Ⓑ Ⓒ Ⓓ   29. Ⓐ Ⓑ Ⓒ Ⓓ
6. Ⓐ Ⓑ Ⓒ Ⓓ   30. Ⓐ Ⓑ Ⓒ Ⓓ
7. Ⓐ Ⓑ Ⓒ Ⓓ   31. Ⓐ Ⓑ Ⓒ Ⓓ
8. Ⓐ Ⓑ Ⓒ Ⓓ   32. Ⓐ Ⓑ Ⓒ Ⓓ
9. Ⓐ Ⓑ Ⓒ Ⓓ   33. Ⓐ Ⓑ Ⓒ Ⓓ
10. Ⓐ Ⓑ Ⓒ Ⓓ   34. Ⓐ Ⓑ Ⓒ Ⓓ
11. Ⓐ Ⓑ Ⓒ Ⓓ   35. Ⓐ Ⓑ Ⓒ Ⓓ
12. Ⓐ Ⓑ Ⓒ Ⓓ   36. Ⓐ Ⓑ Ⓒ Ⓓ
13. Ⓐ Ⓑ Ⓒ Ⓓ   37. Ⓐ Ⓑ Ⓒ Ⓓ
14. Ⓐ Ⓑ Ⓒ Ⓓ
15. Ⓐ Ⓑ Ⓒ Ⓓ
16. Ⓐ Ⓑ Ⓒ Ⓓ
17. Ⓐ Ⓑ Ⓒ Ⓓ
18. Ⓐ Ⓑ Ⓒ Ⓓ
19. Ⓐ Ⓑ Ⓒ Ⓓ
20. Ⓐ Ⓑ Ⓒ Ⓓ
21. Ⓐ Ⓑ Ⓒ Ⓓ
22. Ⓐ Ⓑ Ⓒ Ⓓ
23. Ⓐ Ⓑ Ⓒ Ⓓ
24. Ⓐ Ⓑ Ⓒ Ⓓ

Mathematics Achievement

1. Ⓐ Ⓑ Ⓒ Ⓓ   25. Ⓐ Ⓑ Ⓒ Ⓓ
2. Ⓐ Ⓑ Ⓒ Ⓓ   26. Ⓐ Ⓑ Ⓒ Ⓓ
3. Ⓐ Ⓑ Ⓒ Ⓓ   27. Ⓐ Ⓑ Ⓒ Ⓓ
4. Ⓐ Ⓑ Ⓒ Ⓓ   28. Ⓐ Ⓑ Ⓒ Ⓓ
5. Ⓐ Ⓑ Ⓒ Ⓓ   29. Ⓐ Ⓑ Ⓒ Ⓓ
6. Ⓐ Ⓑ Ⓒ Ⓓ   30. Ⓐ Ⓑ Ⓒ Ⓓ
7. Ⓐ Ⓑ Ⓒ Ⓓ   31. Ⓐ Ⓑ Ⓒ Ⓓ
8. Ⓐ Ⓑ Ⓒ Ⓓ   32. Ⓐ Ⓑ Ⓒ Ⓓ
9. Ⓐ Ⓑ Ⓒ Ⓓ   33. Ⓐ Ⓑ Ⓒ Ⓓ
10. Ⓐ Ⓑ Ⓒ Ⓓ   34. Ⓐ Ⓑ Ⓒ Ⓓ
11. Ⓐ Ⓑ Ⓒ Ⓓ   35. Ⓐ Ⓑ Ⓒ Ⓓ
12. Ⓐ Ⓑ Ⓒ Ⓓ   36. Ⓐ Ⓑ Ⓒ Ⓓ
13. Ⓐ Ⓑ Ⓒ Ⓓ   37. Ⓐ Ⓑ Ⓒ Ⓓ
14. Ⓐ Ⓑ Ⓒ Ⓓ   38. Ⓐ Ⓑ Ⓒ Ⓓ
15. Ⓐ Ⓑ Ⓒ Ⓓ   39. Ⓐ Ⓑ Ⓒ Ⓓ
16. Ⓐ Ⓑ Ⓒ Ⓓ   40. Ⓐ Ⓑ Ⓒ Ⓓ
17. Ⓐ Ⓑ Ⓒ Ⓓ   41. Ⓐ Ⓑ Ⓒ Ⓓ
18. Ⓐ Ⓑ Ⓒ Ⓓ   42. Ⓐ Ⓑ Ⓒ Ⓓ
19. Ⓐ Ⓑ Ⓒ Ⓓ   43. Ⓐ Ⓑ Ⓒ Ⓓ
20. Ⓐ Ⓑ Ⓒ Ⓓ   44. Ⓐ Ⓑ Ⓒ Ⓓ
21. Ⓐ Ⓑ Ⓒ Ⓓ   45. Ⓐ Ⓑ Ⓒ Ⓓ
22. Ⓐ Ⓑ Ⓒ Ⓓ   46. Ⓐ Ⓑ Ⓒ Ⓓ
23. Ⓐ Ⓑ Ⓒ Ⓓ   47. Ⓐ Ⓑ Ⓒ Ⓓ
24. Ⓐ Ⓑ Ⓒ Ⓓ

ISEE Upper Level

Practice Test 3

Part 1 (Quantitative Reasoning)

37 questions

Total time for this section: 35 Minutes

You may NOT use a calculator for this test.

1) If $2y + 6 < 30$, then y could be equal to?
   A. 15
   B. 14
   C. 12
   D. 8

2) Which of the following is NOT a factor of 90?
   A. 9
   B. 10
   C. 16
   D. 30

3) What is the area of a square whose diagonal is 6 meters?
   A. $20\ m^2$
   B. $18\ m^2$
   C. $12\ m^2$
   D. $10\ m^2$

4) If Emily left a $13.26 tip on a breakfast that cost $58.56, approximately what percentage was the tip?
   A. 24%
   B. 22%
   C. 20%
   D. 18%

5) There are 7 blue marbles, 9 red marbles, and 6 yellow marbles in a box. If Ava randomly selects a marble from the box, what is the probability of selecting a red or yellow marble?
   A. $\frac{1}{7}$
   B. $\frac{1}{9}$
   C. $\frac{15}{22}$
   D. $\frac{5}{7}$

6) James earns $8.50 per hour and worked 20 hours. Jacob earns $10.00 per hour. How many hours would Jacob need to work to equal James's earnings over 20 hours?
   A. 14
   B. 17
   C. 20
   D. 25

7) A phone company charges $5 for the first five minutes of a phone call and 50 cents per minute thereafter. If Sofia makes a phone call that lasts 30 minutes, what will be the total cost of the phone call?

A. 18.00

B. 18.50

C. 20.00

D. 20.50

8) Michelle and Alec can finish a job together in 50 minutes. If Michelle can do the job by herself in 2.5 hours, how many minutes does it take Alec to finish the job?

A. 100

B. 75

C. 50

D. 40

9) If 150% of a number is 75, then what is the 90% of that number?

A. 45

B. 50

C. 60

D. 70

10) In the figure, MN is 50 cm. How long is ON?

A. 35 cm

B. 30 cm

C. 25 cm

D. 20 cm

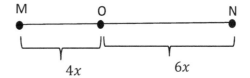

11) On a map, the length of the road from City A to City B is measured to be 18 inches. On this map, $\frac{1}{2}$ inch represents an actual distance of 14 miles. What is the actual distance, in miles, from City A to City B along this road?

A. 504 miles

B. 620 miles

C. 860 miles

D. 1,260 miles

A library has 700 books that include Mathematics, Physics, Chemistry, English and History. Use following graph to answer questions 12.

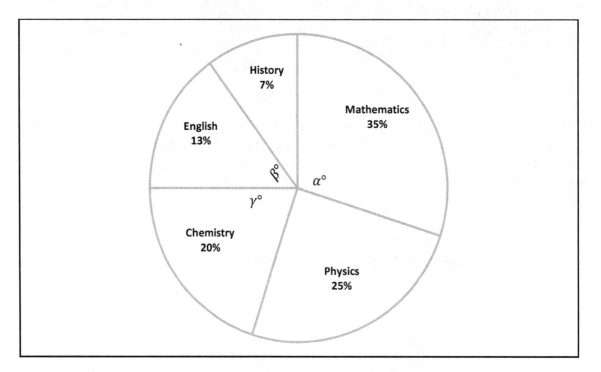

12) What is the product of the number of Mathematics and number of English books?
A. 10,870
B. 18,452
C. 22,295
D. 35,265

13) How many $\frac{1}{6}$ pound paperback books together weigh 60 pounds?
A. 100
B. 200
C. 300
D. 360

14) Emily and Daniel have taken the same number of photos on their school trip. Emily has taken 6 times as many as photos as Claire and Daniel has taken 15 more photos than Claire. How many photos has Claire taken?
A. 2
B. 3
C. 9
D. 11

15) The first four terms in a sequence are shown below. What is the sixth term in the sequence?
$$\{3, 6, 11, 18, \dots\}$$

 A. 38
 B. 40
 C. 45
 D. 50

16) What is the equation of the line that passes through $(3, -3)$ and has a slope of 2?
A. $y = 2x - 9$
B. $y = 3x - 3$
C. $y = 2x + 3$
D. $y = 3x + 9$

17) Find the solution (x, y) to the following system of equations?
$$-4x - y = 8$$
$$8x + 6y = 20$$

 A. $(5, 14)$
 B. $(8, 6)$
 C. $(17, 11)$
 D. $(-\frac{17}{4}, 9)$

18) Sophia purchased a sofa for $530.20. The sofa is regularly priced at $631. What was the percent discount Sophia received on the sofa?

 A. 12%
 B. 16%
 C. 21%
 D. 26%

19) Three second of 20 is equal to $\frac{5}{2}$ of what number?

 A. 12
 B. 20
 C. 40
 D. 60

20) A supermarket's sales increased by 11 percent in the month of April and decreased by 11 percent in the month of May. What is the percent change in the sales of the supermarket over the two-month period?
A. 2% decrease
B. No change
C. 2% increase
D. 2.2% increase

21) The distance between cities A and B is approximately 2,700 miles. If Alice drives an average of 74 miles per hour, how many hours will it take Alice to drive from city A to city B?
A. *Approximately* 41 *hours*
B. *Approximately* 36 *hours*
C. *Approximately* 28 *hours*
D. *Approximately* 21 *hours*

Quantitative Comparisons

Direction: Questions 22 to 37 are Quantitative Comparisons Questions. Using the information provided in each question, compare the quantity in column A to the quantity in Column B. Choose on your answer sheet grid

    A   if the quantity in Column A is greater
    B   if the quantity in Column B is greater
    C   if the two quantities are equal
    D   if the relationship cannot be determined from the information given

22) $x^2 = 8$

Column A	Column B
x	2

23) For all numbers x and y, let the function $x \diamondsuit y$ be defined by $x \diamondsuit y = x^2 - 2xy + y^2$

Column A	Column B
$4 \diamondsuit 5$	$5 \diamondsuit 4$

24)

Column A	Column B
The average of $16, 22, 24, 36, 40$	The average of $28, 33, 38, 42$

25)

Column A	Column B
$\dfrac{1}{x+1}$	$\dfrac{2}{x+2}$

26) $\dfrac{x}{3} = y^2$

Column A	Column B
x	y

27) $x = 1$

Column A	Column B
$2x^3 - 3x - 2$	$3x^2 - 2x - 3$

28)

Column A	Column B
$8 + 14(7 - 3)$	$14 + 8(7 - 3)$

29) $\dfrac{x}{36} = \dfrac{3}{4}$

Column A	Column B
$\dfrac{9}{x}$	$\dfrac{1}{9}$

30) Working at constant rates, machine D makes b rolls of steel in 38 minutes and machine E makes b rolls of steel in one hour ($b > 0$)

Column A	Column B
The number of rolls of steel made by machine D in 3 hours and 10 minutes.	The number of rolls of steel made by machine E in 5 hours.

31) $-1 < y < 4$

Column A	Column B
$\dfrac{y}{2}$	$\dfrac{2}{y}$

32) $\dfrac{a}{b} = \dfrac{c}{d}$

Column A	Column B
$a + b$	$c + d$

33) The ratio of boys to girls in a class is 5 to 7.

Column A	Column B
Ratio of boys to the entire class	$\dfrac{1}{3}$

34) There are only 4 blue marbles and 5 green marbles in a jar. Two marbles are pulled out in succession without replacing them in the jar.

Column A	Column B
The probability that both marbles are blue.	The probability that the first marbles is green, but the second is blue.

35) A magazine printer consecutively numbered the pages of a magazine, starting with 1 on the first page, 10 on the tenth page, etc. In numbering the gages, the printer printed a total of 195 digits.

Column A	Column B
The number of pages in the magazine	100

36)

Column A	Column B
The largest number that can be written by rearranging the digits in 381	The largest number that can be written by rearranging the digits in 279

37) A computer priced $147 includes 5% profit

Column A	Column B
$141	The original cost of the computer

IF YOU FINISH BEFORE TIME IS CALLED, YOU MAY CHECK YOUR WORK ON THIS SECTION ONLY. DO NOT TURN TO ANY OTHER SECTION IN THE TEST.

STOP

ISEE Upper Level

Practice Test 3

Part 2 (Mathematics Achievement)

47 questions

Total time for this section: 40 Minutes

You may NOT use a calculator for this test.

1) How is this number written in scientific notation?

$$0.00003379$$

A. 3.379×10^{-5}

B. 33.79×10^{6}

C. 0.3379×10^{-4}

D. 3379×10^{-8}

2) $|10 - (12 \div |1 - 5|)| = ?$

A. 7

B. -7

C. 5

D. -5

3) $(x + 4)(x + 5) =$

A. $x^2 + 9x + 20$

B. $2x + 12x + 12$

C. $x^2 + 25x + 10$

D. $x^2 + 12x + 35$

4) Find all values of x for which $6x^2 + 16\,x + 8 = 0$

A. $-\dfrac{3}{2}, -\dfrac{1}{2}$

B. $-\dfrac{2}{3}, -2$

C. $-2, -\dfrac{1}{4}$

D. $-\dfrac{2}{3}, \dfrac{1}{2}$

5) Which of the following graphs represents the compound inequality $-2 \le 2x - 4 < 8$?

A.

B.

C.

D.

6) $1 - 9 \div (4^2 \div 2) =$ ___

A. 6

B. $\dfrac{3}{4}$

C. $-\dfrac{1}{8}$

D. -2

7) A girl 200 cm tall, stands 460 cm from a lamp post at night. Her shadow from the light is 80 cm long. How high is the lamp post?

A. 440

B. 500

C. 900

D. 1350

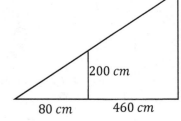

200 cm

80 cm 460 cm

8) Which graph corresponds to the following inequalities?

$$y \leq x + 4$$

$$2x + y \leq -4$$

☐A.

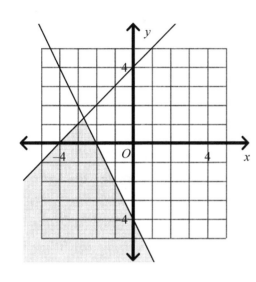

☐B.

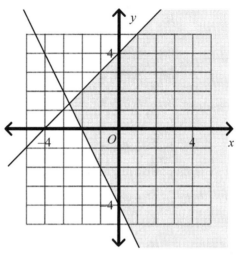

☐C.

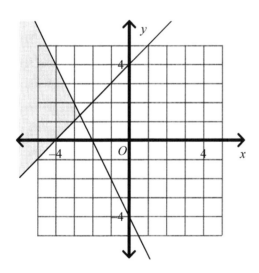

☐D.

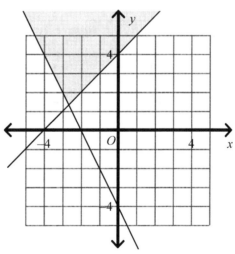

9) The ratio of boys to girls in a school is $3:5$. If there are 600 students in a school, how many boys are in the school?

A. 200

B. 225

C. 300

D. 340

10) $90 \div \frac{1}{9} = ?$

A. 9.125

B. 10

C. 81

D. 810

11) The rectangle on the coordinate grid is translated 5 units down and 4 units to the left.

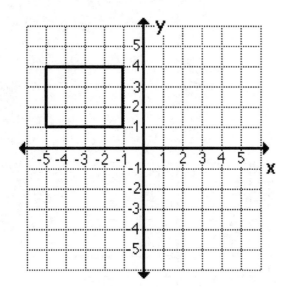

Which of the following describes this transformation?

A. $(x, y) \Rightarrow (x - 4, y + 5)$

B. $(x, y) \Rightarrow (x - 4, y - 5)$

C. $(x, y) \Rightarrow (x + 4, y + 5)$

D. $(x, y) \Rightarrow (x + 4, y - 5)$

12) Find the area of a rectangle with a length of 148 feet and a width of 90 feet.

A. $13,320 \, sq. ft$
B. $13,454 \, sq. ft$
C. $13,404 \, sq. ft$
D. $13,204 \, sq. ft$

13) Which value of x makes the following inequality true?

$$\frac{4}{23} \leq x < 25\%$$

A. 0.12
B. $\dfrac{5}{36}$
C. $\sqrt{0.044}$
D. 0.104

14) Which of the following could be the product of two consecutive prime numbers?

A. 2
B. 10
C. 14
D. 15

15) The perimeter of the trapezoid below is $36 \, cm$. What is its area?

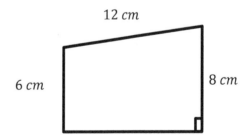

A. $576 \, cm^2$
B. $70 \, cm^2$
C. $48 \, cm^2$
D. $24 cm^2$

16) Emily lives $4\frac{1}{5}$ miles from where she works. When traveling to work, she walks to a bus stop $\frac{1}{2}$ of the way to catch a bus. How many miles away from her house is the bus stop?

A. $2\frac{1}{10}$ *miles*

B. $4\frac{3}{10}$ *miles*

C. $2\frac{3}{10}$ *miles*

D. $1\frac{3}{10}$ *miles*

17) If a vehicle is driven 40 miles on Monday, 45 miles on Tuesday, and 50 miles on Wednesday, what is the average number of miles driven each day?

A. 40 *miles*

B. 45 *miles*

C. 50 *miles*

D. 53 *miles*

18) Use the diagram below to answer the question.

Given the lengths of the base and diagonal of the rectangle below, what is the length of height h, in terms of s?

A. $s\sqrt{2}$

B. $2s\sqrt{2}$

C. $3s$

D. $3s^2$

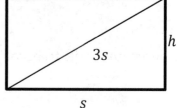

Use the chart below to answer the question.

Color	Number
White	40
Black	30
Beige	40

19) There are also purple marbles in the bag. Which of the following can NOT be the probability of randomly selecting a purple marble from the bag?

A. $\frac{1}{11}$

B. $\frac{1}{6}$

C. $\frac{2}{5}$

D. $\frac{1}{23}$

20) With an 23% discount, Ella was able to save $21.87 on a dress. What was the original price of the dress?

A. $89.92
B. $91.82
C. $95.09
D. $97.92

21) $\frac{8}{35}$ is equals to:

A. 0.28
B. 2.28
C. 0.028
D. 0.228

22) If 30% of A is 1,200, what is 12% of A?

A. 280
B. 480
C. 1,200
D. 1600

23) Simplify $\dfrac{\frac{1}{3} - \frac{x-5}{9}}{\frac{x^3}{3} - \frac{7}{3}}$

A. $\dfrac{7 + x}{3x^3 + 21}$

B. $\dfrac{-7 - x}{x^3 - 21}$

C. $\dfrac{7 + x}{x^3 - 21}$

D. $\dfrac{7 - x}{3x^3 - 21}$

24) If $(6.2 + 8.3 + 2.4) \times x = x$, then what is the value of x?

A. 0
B. $\dfrac{3}{10}$
C. -6
D. -12

25) Two dice are thrown simultaneously, what is the probability of getting a sum of 5 or 8?

A. $\frac{1}{3}$

B. $\frac{1}{4}$

C. $\frac{1}{16}$

D. $\frac{11}{36}$

26) If 7 garbage trucks can collect the trash of 38 homes in a day. How many trucks are needed to collect in 190 houses?

A. 20
B. 30
C. 35
D. 40

27) $78.56 \div 0.05 = ?$

A. 15.712
B. 1,571.2
C. 157.12
D. 1.5712

28) In the following figure, AB is the diameter of the circle. What is the circumference of the circle?

A. 4π
B. 6π
C. 8π
D. 10π

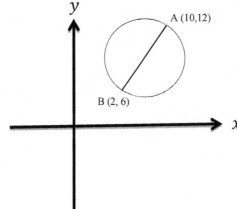

29) What is the value of x in the following equation?
$$2x^2 + 6 = 26$$

A. ± 4
B. $\pm \sqrt{9}$
C. $\pm \sqrt{10}$
D. ± 3

30) A circle has a diameter of 20 inches. What is its approximate area?

A. $314 \ inch^2$
B. $114 \ inch^2$
C. $74.00 \ inch^2$
D. $12.56 \ inch^2$

31) $6 \ days \ 20 \ hours \ 36 \ minutes - 4 \ days \ 12 \ hours \ 24 \ minutes \ = ?$

A. $2 \ days \ 8 \ hours \ 12 \ minutes$
B. $1 \ days \ 8 \ hours \ 12 \ minutes$
C. $2 \ days \ 7 \ hours \ 14 \ minutes$
D. $1 \ days \ 7 \ hours \ 14 \ minutes$

32) The base of a right triangle is 4 feet, and the interior angles are $45 - 45 - 90$. What is its area?

A. $2 \ square \ feet$
B. $4 \ square \ feet$
C. $8 \ square \ feet$
D. $10 \ square \ feet$

Use the following table to answer question below.

DANIEL'S BIRD-WATCHING PROJECT	
DAY	NUMBER OF RAPTORS SEEN
Monday	?
Tuesday	10
Wednesday	15
Thursday	13
Friday	6
MEAN	11

33) The above table shows the data Daniel collects while watching birds for one week. How many raptors did Daniel see on Monday?

A. 10
B. 11
C. 12
D. 13

34) A floppy disk shows 837,036 bytes free and 639,352 bytes used. If you delete a file of size 542,159 bytes and create a new file of size 499,986 bytes, how many free bytes will the floppy disk have?

A. 567,179 bytes
B. 671,525 bytes
C. 879,209 bytes
D. 899,209 bytes

35) Increased by 40%, the number 70 becomes:

A. 40
B. 98
C. 126
D. 130

36) If $12 + x^{\frac{1}{2}} = 24$, then what is the value of $5 \times x$?
   A. 15
   B. 60
   C. 240
   D. 720

37) Which equation represents the statement "twice the difference between 5 times H and 2 gives 35".
   A. $\frac{5H + 2}{2} = 35$
   B. $5(2H + 2) = 35$
   C. $2(5H - 2) = 35$
   D. $2\frac{5H}{2} = 35$

38) A circle is inscribed in a square, as shown below.

The area of the circle is $25\pi \ cm^2$ What is the area of the square?

   A) $10 \ cm^2$
   B) $26 \ cm^2$
   C) $48 \ cm^2$
   D) $100 \ cm^2$

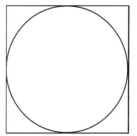

39) Triangle ABC is graphed on a coordinate grid with vertices at $A \ (-2, -3)$, $B \ (-4, 1)$ and $C \ (9, 7)$. Triangle ABC is reflected over x axes to create triangle $A'B'C'$.

Which order pair represents the coordinate of C'?
   A. $(9, 7)$
   B. $(-9, -7)$
   C. $(9, -7)$
   D. $(7, -9)$

40) Which set of ordered pairs represents y as a function of x?
   A. $\{(5, -2), (5, 7), (9, -8), (4, -7)\}$
   B. $\{(2, 2), (3, -9), (5, 8), (2, 7)\}$
   C. $\{(9, 12), (8, 7), (6, 11), (8, 18)\}$
   D. $\{(6, 1), (3, 1), (0, 5), (6, 1)\}$

41) The width of a box is one third of its length. The height of the box is one half of its width. If the length of the box is 24 cm, what is the volume of the box?

A. $80cm^3$
B. $165\ cm^3$
C. $243\ cm^3$
D. $768cm^3$

42) How many 4×4 squares can fit inside a rectangle with a height of 40 and width of 12?

A. 60
B. 50
C. 40
D. 30

43) David makes a weekly salary of $230 plus 9% commission on his sales. What will his income be for a week in which he makes sales totaling $1,200?

A. $338
B. $318
C. $308
D. $298

44) $5x^3y^2 + 4x^5y^3 - (6x^3y^2 - 4xy^5) =$ ___

A. $4x^5y^3$
B. $4x^5y^3 - x^3y^2 + 4xy^5$
C. $C.x^3y^2$
D. $4x^5y^3 - x^3y^2$

45) The radius of circle A is five times the radius of circle B. If the circumference of circle A is 20π, what is the area of circle B?

A. 3π
B. 4π
C. 6π
D. 12π

46) A square measures 8 inches on one side. By how much will the area be decreased if its length is increased by 5 inches and its width decreased by 4 inches.

A. $1\ sq\ decreased$
B. $3\ sq\ decreased$
C. $8\ sq\ decreased$
D. $12\ sq\ decreased$

47) If a box contains red and blue balls in ratio of $3:2$ red to blue, how many red balls are there if 80 blue balls are in the box?

A. 60
B. 80
C. 100
D. 120

IF YOU FINISH BEFORE TIME IS CALLED, YOU MAY CHECK YOUR WORK ON THIS SECTION.

STOP

ISEE Upper Level Math Practice Test 4

2019 - 2020

Two Parts

Total number of questions: 84

Part 1 (Calculator): 37 questions

Part 2 (Calculator): 47 questions

Total time for two parts: 75 Minutes

ISEE Upper Level Practice Test Answer Sheets

Remove (or photocopy) this answer sheet and use it to complete the practice test.

ISEE Upper Level Practice Test 4			
Quantitative Reasoning		**Mathematics Achievement**	

Quantitative Reasoning

1 Ⓐ Ⓑ Ⓒ Ⓓ   25 Ⓐ Ⓑ Ⓒ Ⓓ
2 Ⓐ Ⓑ Ⓒ Ⓓ   26 Ⓐ Ⓑ Ⓒ Ⓓ
3 Ⓐ Ⓑ Ⓒ Ⓓ   27 Ⓐ Ⓑ Ⓒ Ⓓ
4 Ⓐ Ⓑ Ⓒ Ⓓ   28 Ⓐ Ⓑ Ⓒ Ⓓ
5 Ⓐ Ⓑ Ⓒ Ⓓ   29 Ⓐ Ⓑ Ⓒ Ⓓ
6 Ⓐ Ⓑ Ⓒ Ⓓ   30 Ⓐ Ⓑ Ⓒ Ⓓ
7 Ⓐ Ⓑ Ⓒ Ⓓ   31 Ⓐ Ⓑ Ⓒ Ⓓ
8 Ⓐ Ⓑ Ⓒ Ⓓ   32 Ⓐ Ⓑ Ⓒ Ⓓ
9 Ⓐ Ⓑ Ⓒ Ⓓ   33 Ⓐ Ⓑ Ⓒ Ⓓ
10 Ⓐ Ⓑ Ⓒ Ⓓ   34 Ⓐ Ⓑ Ⓒ Ⓓ
11 Ⓐ Ⓑ Ⓒ Ⓓ   35 Ⓐ Ⓑ Ⓒ Ⓓ
12 Ⓐ Ⓑ Ⓒ Ⓓ   36 Ⓐ Ⓑ Ⓒ Ⓓ
13 Ⓐ Ⓑ Ⓒ Ⓓ   37 Ⓐ Ⓑ Ⓒ Ⓓ
14 Ⓐ Ⓑ Ⓒ Ⓓ
15 Ⓐ Ⓑ Ⓒ Ⓓ
16 Ⓐ Ⓑ Ⓒ Ⓓ
17 Ⓐ Ⓑ Ⓒ Ⓓ
18 Ⓐ Ⓑ Ⓒ Ⓓ
19 Ⓐ Ⓑ Ⓒ Ⓓ
20 Ⓐ Ⓑ Ⓒ Ⓓ
21 Ⓐ Ⓑ Ⓒ Ⓓ
22 Ⓐ Ⓑ Ⓒ Ⓓ
23 Ⓐ Ⓑ Ⓒ Ⓓ
24 Ⓐ Ⓑ Ⓒ Ⓓ

Mathematics Achievement

1 Ⓐ Ⓑ Ⓒ Ⓓ   25 Ⓐ Ⓑ Ⓒ Ⓓ
2 Ⓐ Ⓑ Ⓒ Ⓓ   26 Ⓐ Ⓑ Ⓒ Ⓓ
3 Ⓐ Ⓑ Ⓒ Ⓓ   27 Ⓐ Ⓑ Ⓒ Ⓓ
4 Ⓐ Ⓑ Ⓒ Ⓓ   28 Ⓐ Ⓑ Ⓒ Ⓓ
5 Ⓐ Ⓑ Ⓒ Ⓓ   29 Ⓐ Ⓑ Ⓒ Ⓓ
6 Ⓐ Ⓑ Ⓒ Ⓓ   30 Ⓐ Ⓑ Ⓒ Ⓓ
7 Ⓐ Ⓑ Ⓒ Ⓓ   31 Ⓐ Ⓑ Ⓒ Ⓓ
8 Ⓐ Ⓑ Ⓒ Ⓓ   32 Ⓐ Ⓑ Ⓒ Ⓓ
9 Ⓐ Ⓑ Ⓒ Ⓓ   33 Ⓐ Ⓑ Ⓒ Ⓓ
10 Ⓐ Ⓑ Ⓒ Ⓓ   34 Ⓐ Ⓑ Ⓒ Ⓓ
11 Ⓐ Ⓑ Ⓒ Ⓓ   35 Ⓐ Ⓑ Ⓒ Ⓓ
12 Ⓐ Ⓑ Ⓒ Ⓓ   36 Ⓐ Ⓑ Ⓒ Ⓓ
13 Ⓐ Ⓑ Ⓒ Ⓓ   37 Ⓐ Ⓑ Ⓒ Ⓓ
14 Ⓐ Ⓑ Ⓒ Ⓓ   38 Ⓐ Ⓑ Ⓒ Ⓓ
15 Ⓐ Ⓑ Ⓒ Ⓓ   39 Ⓐ Ⓑ Ⓒ Ⓓ
16 Ⓐ Ⓑ Ⓒ Ⓓ   40 Ⓐ Ⓑ Ⓒ Ⓓ
17 Ⓐ Ⓑ Ⓒ Ⓓ   41 Ⓐ Ⓑ Ⓒ Ⓓ
18 Ⓐ Ⓑ Ⓒ Ⓓ   42 Ⓐ Ⓑ Ⓒ Ⓓ
19 Ⓐ Ⓑ Ⓒ Ⓓ   43 Ⓐ Ⓑ Ⓒ Ⓓ
20 Ⓐ Ⓑ Ⓒ Ⓓ   44 Ⓐ Ⓑ Ⓒ Ⓓ
21 Ⓐ Ⓑ Ⓒ Ⓓ   45 Ⓐ Ⓑ Ⓒ Ⓓ
22 Ⓐ Ⓑ Ⓒ Ⓓ   46 Ⓐ Ⓑ Ⓒ Ⓓ
23 Ⓐ Ⓑ Ⓒ Ⓓ   47 Ⓐ Ⓑ Ⓒ Ⓓ
24 Ⓐ Ⓑ Ⓒ Ⓓ

ISEE Upper Level

Practice Test 4

Part 1 (Quantitative Reasoning)

37 questions

Total time for this section: 35 Minutes

You may NOT use a calculator for this test.

1) How much greater is the value of $4x + 9$ than the value of $4x - 3$?

A. 8
B. 10
C. 12
D. 14

2) What is the prime factorization of 1,400?

A. $2 \times 2 \times 5 \times 5$
B. $2 \times 2 \times 2 \times 5 \times 5 \times 7$
C. 2×5
D. $2 \times 2 \times 2 \times 5 \times 7$

3) If 6 inches on a map represents an actual distance of 150 feet, then what actual distance does 20 inches on the map represent?

A. 180 feet
B. 200 feet
C. 250 feet
D. 500 feet

4) The circle graph below shows all Mr. Green's expenses for last month. If he spent $550 on his car, how much did he spend for his rent?

A. $675
B. $750
C. $780
D. $810

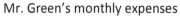
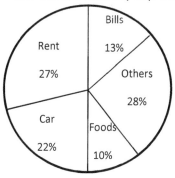

Mr. Green's monthly expenses

5) The area of a circle is less than 49π. Which of the following can be the circumference of the circle?

A. 10π
B. 14π
C. 24π
D. 32π

6) A basket contains 25 balls and the average weight of each of these balls is 35 g. The five heaviest balls have an average weight of 50 g each. If we remove the three heaviest balls from the basket, what is the average weight of the remaining balls?

A. 10 g

B. 20.25 g

C. 31.25 g

D. 35 g

7) If $f(x) = x^2 + 6$, what is the smallest possible value of $f(x)$?

A. 0

B. 5

C. 6

D. 7

8) Alice drives from her house to work at an average speed of 45 miles per hour and she drives at an average speed of 65 miles per hour when she was returning home. What was her minimum speed on the round trip in miles per hour?

A. 45

B. 58.5

C. 65

D. Cannot be determined

9) If the sum of the positive integers from 1 to n is 3,350, and the sum of the positive integers from $n + 1$ to $2n$ is 4,866, which of the following represents the sum of the positive integers from 1 to $2n$ inclusive?

A. 3,350

B. 4,866

C. 7,000

D. 8,216

10) Oscar purchased a new hat that was on sale for $8.34. The original price was $14.65. What percentage discount was the sale price?

A. 4.2%

B. 40.5%

C. 43%

D. 45%

11) Which of the following statements is correct, according to the graph below?

Number of Books Sold in a Bookstore

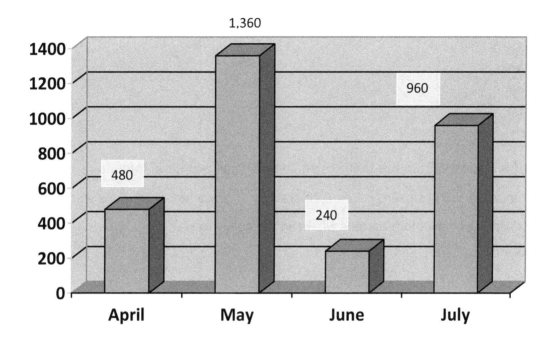

A. Number of books sold in April was twice the number of books sold in July.

B. Number of books sold in July was less than half the number of books sold in May.

C. Number of books sold in June was half the number of books sold in April.

D. Number of books sold in July was equal to the number of books sold in April plus the number of books sold in June.

12) List A consists of the numbers $\{2, 4, 9, 11, 16\}$, and list B consists of the numbers $\{5, 7, 13, 15, 18\}$.
If the two lists are combined, what is the median of the combined list?

A. 7

B. 8

C. 9

D. 10

13) A bag contains 19 balls: three green, five black, eight blue, a brown, a red and one white. If 17 balls are removed from the bag at random, what is the probability that a brown ball has been removed?

A. $\dfrac{1}{9}$

B. $\dfrac{1}{6}$

C. $\dfrac{16}{19}$

D. $\dfrac{17}{19}$

14) If Jim adds 150 stamps to his current stamp collection, the total number of stamps will be equal to $\dfrac{4}{3}$ the current number of stamps. If Jim adds 40% more stamps to the current collection, how many stamps will be in the collection?

A. 340

B. 453

C. 512

D. 630

15) If $x + y = 7$ and $x - y = 6$ then what is the value of $(x^2 - y^2)$?

A. 24

B. 42

C. 65

D. 90

16) The area of rectangle $ABCD$ is 108 square inches. If the length of the rectangle is three times the width, what is the perimeter of rectangle $ABCD$?

A. 48 inches

B. 67 inches

C. 76 inches

D. 86 inches

17) What's The ratio of boys and girls in a class is $7:4$. If there are 55 students in the class, how many more girls should be enrolled to make the ratio $1:1$?

A. 6

B. 10

C. 12

D. 15

18) The sum of 8 numbers is greater than 320 and less than 480. Which of the following could be the average (arithmetic mean) of the numbers?

A. 30
B. 35
C. 40
D. 45

19) A gas tank can hold 35 gallons when it is $\frac{5}{2}$ full. How many gallons does it contain when it is full?

A. 125
B. 62.5
C. 50
D. 14

20) Triangle ABC is similar to triangle ADE. What is the length of side EC?

A. 4
B. 10
C. 18
D. 45

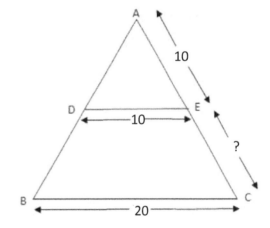

21) Which of the following expressions gives the value of b in terms of f, c, and z from the following equation?

$$f = [\frac{cz}{b}]^2$$

A. $b = fc^2z^2$
B. $b = \frac{cz}{\sqrt{f}}$
C. $b = \frac{\sqrt{f}}{cz}$
D. $b = [\frac{cz}{f}]^2$

Quantitative Comparisons

Direction: Questions 22 to 37 are Quantitative Comparisons Questions. Using the information provided in each question, compare the quantity in column A to the quantity in Column B. Choose on your answer sheet grid

A   if the quantity in Column A is greater

B   if the quantity in Column B is greater

C   if the two quantities are equal

D   if the relationship cannot be determined from the information given

22)

Column A	Column B
5^2	$\sqrt[3]{125}$

23)

Column A	Column B
7	$(52)^{\frac{1}{2}}$

24)

Column A	Column B
The average of $21, 29,$ and 37	28

25)

Column A	Column B
$16 \times 435 \times 25$	$19 \times 435 \times 22$

26) x is an integer

Column A	Column B
$-x$	$\dfrac{x}{3}$

27)

Column A	Column B
$(\dfrac{1}{4})^3$	4^{-3}

28) $3x + 7 > x - 1$

Column A	Column B
x	-7

29)

Column A	Column B
The greatest value of x in	The greatest value of x in
$8\,\lvert 3x - 2 \rvert = 16$	$8\,\lvert 3x - 2 \rvert = 16$

30) x is an integer

Column A	Column B
$(x)^5(x)^2$	$(x^5)^2$

31)

Column A	Column B
The probability that	The probability that
event x will occur.	event x will not occur.

32) The selling price of a sport jacket including 20% discount is $68.

Column A	Column B
Original price of the sport jacket	$80

33) $x^2 - 2x - 20 = 15$

Column A	Column B
x	5

34)

Column A	Column B
$(0.82)^{28}$	$(0.82)^{27}$

35)

Column A	Column B
The probability of rolling a 4 on a die and getting heads on a coin toss.	The probability of rolling an odd number on a die and picking a spade from a deck of 52 cards.

36)

Column A	Column B
$0.46	Sum of one quarter, three nickels, and three pennies

37) x is an odd integer, and y is an even integer. In a certain game an odd number is considered greater than an even number.

Column A	Column B
$x(x + y)$	$(x - y) - y^2$

IF YOU FINISH BEFORE TIME IS CALLED, YOU MAY CHECK YOUR WORK ON THIS SECTION.

STOP

ISEE Upper Level

Practice Test 4

Part 2 (Mathematics Achievement)

47 questions

Total time for this section: 40 Minutes

You may NOT use a calculator for this test.

1) Which of the following points lies on the line $4x + 6y = 20$?
A. $(2, 1)$
B. $(-1, 3)$
C. $(-2, 2)$
D. $(2, 2)$

2) 5 less than twice a positive integer is 91. What is the integer?
A. 40
B. 41
C. 42
D. 48

3) If $\frac{|3+x|}{5} \leq 8$, then which of the following is correct?
A. $-43 \leq x \leq 37$
B. $-43 \leq x \leq 32$
C. $-32 \leq x \leq 38$
D. $-32 \leq x \leq 32$

4) $\frac{1}{5b^2} + \frac{1}{5b} = \frac{1}{b^2}$, then $= ?$
A. $-\frac{16}{5}$
B. 4
C. $-\frac{5}{16}$
D. 8

5) An angle is equal to one ninth of its supplement. What is the measure of that angle?
A. $18°$
B. $40°$
C. $60°$
D. $80°$

6) 1.3 is what percent of 26?
A. 1.3
B. 5
C. 18
D. 24

7) The cost, in thousands of dollars, of producing x thousands of textbooks is $C(x) = x^2 + 2x$. The revenue, also in thousands of dollars, is $R(x) = 40x$. find the profit or loss if 20 textbooks are produced. ($profit = revenue - cost$)
   A. $2,160 profit
   B. $360 profit
   C. $2,160 loss
   D. $360 loss

8) Simplify $7x^3y^3(2x^3y)^3 =$
   A. $14x^4y^6$
   B. $14x^8y^6$
   C. $56x^{12}y^6$
   D. $56x^8y^6$

9) Ella (E) is 5 years older than her friend Ava (A) who is 4 years younger than her sister Sofia (S). If E, A and S denote their ages, which one of the following represents the given information?

   A. $\begin{cases} E = A + 5 \\ S = A - 4 \end{cases}$
   B. $\begin{cases} E = A + 5 \\ A = S + 4 \end{cases}$
   C. $\begin{cases} A = E + 5 \\ S = A - 4 \end{cases}$
   D. $\begin{cases} E = A + 5 \\ A = S - 4 \end{cases}$

10) Right triangle ABC has two legs of lengths $4\ cm$ (AB) and $3\ cm$ (AC). What is the length of the third side (BC)?
    A. $5\ cm$
    B. $6\ cm$
    C. $9\ cm$
    D. $10\ cm$

11) Which is the longest time?
    A. $24\ hours$
    B. $1,520\ minutes$
    C. $3\ days$
    D. $4,200\ seconds$

12) A circle has a diameter of 10 inches. What is its approximate circumference?
   A. 6.28 inches.
   B. 25.12 inches.
   C. 31.4 inches.
   D. 35.12 inches.

13) Write 623 in expanded form, using exponents.
   A. $(6 \times 10^3) + (2 \times 10^2) + (3 \times 10)$
   B. $(6 \times 10^2) + (2 \times 10^1) - 5$
   C. $(6 \times 10^2) + (2 \times 10^1) + 3$
   D. $(6 \times 10^1) + (2 \times 10^2) + 3$

14) What is the area of an isosceles right triangle with hypotenuse that measures $8 \, cm$?
   A. $9 \, cm^2$
   B. $16 \, cm^2$
   C. $3\sqrt{2} \, cm^2$
   D. $64 \, cm^2$

15) A company pays its writer $5 for every 500 words written. How much will a writer earn for an article with 860 words?
   A. $12
   B. $5.6
   C. $8.6
   D. $10.7

16) A circular logo is enlarged to fit the lid of a jar. The new diameter is 20% larger than the original. By what percentage has the area of the logo increased?
   A. 20%
   B. 44%
   C. 69%
   D. 75%

17) $89.44 \div 0.05 = ?$
   A. 17.888
   B. 1,788.8
   C. 178.88
   D. 1.7888

18) What's the area of the non-shaded part of the following figure?

A. 225

B. 152

C. 40

D. 42

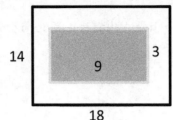

19) A bread recipe calls for $2\frac{1}{2}$ cups of flour. If you only have $1\frac{5}{4}$ cups, how much more flour is needed?

A. 1

B. $\frac{1}{2}$

C. 2

D. $\frac{1}{4}$

20) What is the maximum value for y if $y = -(x-2)^2 + 7$?

A. -7

B. -2

C. 2

D. 7

21) What is the solution of the following system of equations?

$$\begin{cases} -3x - y = -5 \\ 5x - 5y = 15 \end{cases}$$

A. $(-1, 2)$

B. $(2, -1)$

C. $(1, 4)$

D. $(4, -2)$

22) The equation of a line is given as: $y = 5x - 3$. Which of the following points does not lie on the line?

A. $(2, 7)$

B. $(-2, -13)$

C. $(4, 21)$

D. $(-4, -23)$

23) The drivers at G & G trucking must report the mileage on their trucks each week. The mileage reading of Ed's vehicle was 52,806 at the beginning of one week, and 53,431 at the end of the same week. What was the total number of miles driven by Ed that week?

A. 515 *miles*
B. 525 *miles*
C. 625 *miles*
D. 658 *miles*

24) What is the area of an isosceles right triangle that has one leg that measures $4\ cm$?

    A. $8\ cm^2$
    B. $36\ cm^2$
    C. $3\sqrt{2}\ cm^2$
    D. $72\ cm^2$

25) Which of the following is a factor of both $x^2 - 5x + 6$ and $x^2 - 6x + 8$?

    A. $(x - 2)$
    B. $(x + 4)$
    C. $(x + 2)$
    D. $(x - 4)$

26)
$$\begin{array}{r} 36 \text{ hr. } 38 \text{ min.} \\ - 23 \text{ hr. } 25 \text{ min.} \\ \hline \end{array}$$

    A. $12\ hr.\ 57\ min.$
    B. $12\ hr.\ 47\ min.$
    C. $13\ hr.\ 13\ min.$
    D. $13\ hr.\ 57\ min.$

27) $\dfrac{14}{26}$ is equal to:

    A. 5.4
    B. 0.54
    C. 0.05
    D. 0.5

28) If $x + y = 10$, what is the value of $9x + 9y$?

    A. 192
    B. 104
    C. 90
    D. 48

29) What is the number of cubic feet of soil needed for a flower box 2 feet long, 10 inches wide, and 2 feet deep?

    A. 22 cubic feet
    B. 12 cubic feet
    C. $\dfrac{10}{3}$ cubic feet
    D. 2 cubic feet

30) A car uses 20 gallons of gas to travel 460 miles. How many miles per gallon does the car use?

   A. 23 miles per gallon
   B. 32 miles per gallon
   C. 30 miles per gallon
   D. 34 miles per gallon

31) What is the reciprocal of $\frac{x^3}{15}$?

   A. $\frac{15}{x^3} - 1$
   B. $\frac{48}{x^3}$
   C. $\frac{15}{x^3} + 1$
   D. $\frac{15}{x^3}$

32) Karen is 9 years older than her sister Michelle, and Michelle is 4 years younger than her brother David. If the sum of their ages is 91, how old is Michelle?

   A. 21
   B. 26
   C. 28
   D. 29

33) Mario loaned Jett $1,400 at a yearly interest rate of 6%. After one year what is the interest owned on this loan?

   A. $1,260
   B. $140
   C. $84
   D. $30

34) Calculate the area of a parallelogram with a base of 3 feet and height of 3.2 feet.

   A. 2.8 square feet
   B. 4.2 square feet
   C. 5.8 square feet
   D. 9.6 square feet

35) Ellis just got hired for on-the-road sales and will travel about 2,500 miles a week during an 90-hour work week. If the time spent traveling is $\frac{5}{3}$ of his week, how many hours a week will he be on the road?

   A. Ellis spends about 34 hours of his 90-hour work week on the road.
   B. Ellis spends about 40 hours of his 90-hour work week on the road.
   C. Ellis spends about 48 hours of his 90-hour work week on the road.
   D. Ellis spends about 150 hours of his 90-hour work week on the road.

36) Given that $x = 0.5$ and $y = 5$, what is the value of $2x^2(y + 4)$?

   A. 4.5
   B. 8.2
   C. 12.2
   D. 14.2

37) What is the area of the shaded region if the diameter of the bigger circle is 14 inches and the diameter of the smaller circle is 10 inches.

   A. $16\,\pi\ inch^2$
   B. $24\,\pi\ inch^2$
   C. $36\,\pi\ inch^2$
   D. $80\,\pi\ inch^2$

38) A shirt costing $500 is discounted 25%. After a month, the shirt is discounted another 15%. Which of the following expressions can be used to find the selling price of the shirt?
   A. $(500)\,(0.70)$
   B. $(500) - 500\,(0.30)$
   C. $(500)(0.15) - (500)\,(0.15)$
   D. $(500)\,(0.75)\,(0.85)$

39) A tree 40 feet tall casts a shadow 18 feet long. Jack is 5 feet tall. How long is Jack's shadow?
   A. $2.25\ ft$
   B. $4\ ft$
   C. $5.25\ ft$
   D. $7\ ft$

40) In a school, the ratio of number of boys to girls is $7:3$. If the number of boys is 210, what is the total number of students in the school?
   A. 300
   B. 500
   C. 540
   D. 600

41) If x is 35% percent of 620, what is x?

    A. 185
    B. 217
    C. 402
    D. 720

42) How many square feet of tile is needed for a $19\ feet \times 19\ feet$ room?

    A. 72 square feet
    B. 108 square feet
    C. 361 square feet
    D. 416 square feet

43) $(4x + 4)\ (x + 5) =$

    A. $4x + 8$
    B. $4x + 3x + 15$
    C. $4x^2 + 24x + 20$
    D. $4x^2 + 3$

44) If $x\blacksquare y = \sqrt{x^2 + y}$, what is the value of $4\blacksquare 9$?

    A. $\sqrt{126}$
    B. 6
    C. 5
    D. 4

45) There are four equal tanks of water. If $\frac{2}{3}$ of a tank contains 200 liters of water, what is the capacity of the three tanks of water together?

    A. 1,200 liters
    B. 500 liters
    C. 240 liters
    D. 80 liters

46) What is the result of the expression?

$$\begin{vmatrix} 3 & 6 \\ -1 & -3 \\ -5 & -1 \end{vmatrix} + \begin{vmatrix} 2 & -1 \\ 6 & 4 \\ 1 & 3 \end{vmatrix}$$

A. $\begin{vmatrix} 1 & -1 \\ 6 & 0 \\ 2 & 3 \end{vmatrix}$

B. $\begin{vmatrix} 3 & 7 \\ -1 & -3 \\ -5 & -1 \end{vmatrix}$

C. $\begin{vmatrix} 5 & 5 \\ 5 & 1 \\ -4 & 2 \end{vmatrix}$

D. $\begin{vmatrix} 5 & -3 \\ -6 & 1 \\ -10 & -3 \end{vmatrix}$

47) The average weight of 20 girls in a class is 55 kg and the average weight of 35 boys in the same class is 70 kg. What is the average weight of all the 55 students in that class?

A. 60 kg
B. 61.28 kg
C. 64.54 kg
D. 65.9 kg

IF YOU FINISH BEFORE TIME IS CALLED, YOU MAY CHECK YOUR WORK ON THIS SECTION. STOP

ISEE Upper Level Math Practice Test 5

2019 - 2020

Two Parts

Total number of questions: 84

Part 1 (Calculator): 37 questions

Part 2 (Calculator): 47 questions

Total time for two parts: 75 Minutes

ISEE Upper Level Practice Test Answer Sheets

Remove (or photocopy) this answer sheet and use it to complete the practice test.

ISEE Upper Level Practice Test 5		
Quantitative Reasoning		**Mathematics Achievement**

Quantitative Reasoning

1 Ⓐ Ⓑ Ⓒ Ⓓ   25 Ⓐ Ⓑ Ⓒ Ⓓ
2 Ⓐ Ⓑ Ⓒ Ⓓ   26 Ⓐ Ⓑ Ⓒ Ⓓ
3 Ⓐ Ⓑ Ⓒ Ⓓ   27 Ⓐ Ⓑ Ⓒ Ⓓ
4 Ⓐ Ⓑ Ⓒ Ⓓ   28 Ⓐ Ⓑ Ⓒ Ⓓ
5 Ⓐ Ⓑ Ⓒ Ⓓ   29 Ⓐ Ⓑ Ⓒ Ⓓ
6 Ⓐ Ⓑ Ⓒ Ⓓ   30 Ⓐ Ⓑ Ⓒ Ⓓ
7 Ⓐ Ⓑ Ⓒ Ⓓ   31 Ⓐ Ⓑ Ⓒ Ⓓ
8 Ⓐ Ⓑ Ⓒ Ⓓ   32 Ⓐ Ⓑ Ⓒ Ⓓ
9 Ⓐ Ⓑ Ⓒ Ⓓ   33 Ⓐ Ⓑ Ⓒ Ⓓ
10 Ⓐ Ⓑ Ⓒ Ⓓ   34 Ⓐ Ⓑ Ⓒ Ⓓ
11 Ⓐ Ⓑ Ⓒ Ⓓ   35 Ⓐ Ⓑ Ⓒ Ⓓ
12 Ⓐ Ⓑ Ⓒ Ⓓ   36 Ⓐ Ⓑ Ⓒ Ⓓ
13 Ⓐ Ⓑ Ⓒ Ⓓ   37 Ⓐ Ⓑ Ⓒ Ⓓ
14 Ⓐ Ⓑ Ⓒ Ⓓ
15 Ⓐ Ⓑ Ⓒ Ⓓ
16 Ⓐ Ⓑ Ⓒ Ⓓ
17 Ⓐ Ⓑ Ⓒ Ⓓ
18 Ⓐ Ⓑ Ⓒ Ⓓ
19 Ⓐ Ⓑ Ⓒ Ⓓ
20 Ⓐ Ⓑ Ⓒ Ⓓ
21 Ⓐ Ⓑ Ⓒ Ⓓ
22 Ⓐ Ⓑ Ⓒ Ⓓ
23 Ⓐ Ⓑ Ⓒ Ⓓ
24 Ⓐ Ⓑ Ⓒ Ⓓ

Mathematics Achievement

1 Ⓐ Ⓑ Ⓒ Ⓓ   25 Ⓐ Ⓑ Ⓒ Ⓓ
2 Ⓐ Ⓑ Ⓒ Ⓓ   26 Ⓐ Ⓑ Ⓒ Ⓓ
3 Ⓐ Ⓑ Ⓒ Ⓓ   27 Ⓐ Ⓑ Ⓒ Ⓓ
4 Ⓐ Ⓑ Ⓒ Ⓓ   28 Ⓐ Ⓑ Ⓒ Ⓓ
5 Ⓐ Ⓑ Ⓒ Ⓓ   29 Ⓐ Ⓑ Ⓒ Ⓓ
6 Ⓐ Ⓑ Ⓒ Ⓓ   30 Ⓐ Ⓑ Ⓒ Ⓓ
7 Ⓐ Ⓑ Ⓒ Ⓓ   31 Ⓐ Ⓑ Ⓒ Ⓓ
8 Ⓐ Ⓑ Ⓒ Ⓓ   32 Ⓐ Ⓑ Ⓒ Ⓓ
9 Ⓐ Ⓑ Ⓒ Ⓓ   33 Ⓐ Ⓑ Ⓒ Ⓓ
10 Ⓐ Ⓑ Ⓒ Ⓓ   34 Ⓐ Ⓑ Ⓒ Ⓓ
11 Ⓐ Ⓑ Ⓒ Ⓓ   35 Ⓐ Ⓑ Ⓒ Ⓓ
12 Ⓐ Ⓑ Ⓒ Ⓓ   36 Ⓐ Ⓑ Ⓒ Ⓓ
13 Ⓐ Ⓑ Ⓒ Ⓓ   37 Ⓐ Ⓑ Ⓒ Ⓓ
14 Ⓐ Ⓑ Ⓒ Ⓓ   38 Ⓐ Ⓑ Ⓒ Ⓓ
15 Ⓐ Ⓑ Ⓒ Ⓓ   39 Ⓐ Ⓑ Ⓒ Ⓓ
16 Ⓐ Ⓑ Ⓒ Ⓓ   40 Ⓐ Ⓑ Ⓒ Ⓓ
17 Ⓐ Ⓑ Ⓒ Ⓓ   41 Ⓐ Ⓑ Ⓒ Ⓓ
18 Ⓐ Ⓑ Ⓒ Ⓓ   42 Ⓐ Ⓑ Ⓒ Ⓓ
19 Ⓐ Ⓑ Ⓒ Ⓓ   43 Ⓐ Ⓑ Ⓒ Ⓓ
20 Ⓐ Ⓑ Ⓒ Ⓓ   44 Ⓐ Ⓑ Ⓒ Ⓓ
21 Ⓐ Ⓑ Ⓒ Ⓓ   45 Ⓐ Ⓑ Ⓒ Ⓓ
22 Ⓐ Ⓑ Ⓒ Ⓓ   46 Ⓐ Ⓑ Ⓒ Ⓓ
23 Ⓐ Ⓑ Ⓒ Ⓓ   47 Ⓐ Ⓑ Ⓒ Ⓓ
24 Ⓐ Ⓑ Ⓒ Ⓓ

ISEE Upper Level

Practice Test 5

Part 1 (Quantitative Reasoning)

37 questions

Total time for this section: 35 Minutes

You may NOT use a calculator for this test.

1) What is the prime factorization of 280?

   A. $2 \times 2 \times 5 \times 7$
   B. $2 \times 2 \times 2 \times 2 \times 5 \times 7$
   C. 2×7
   D. $2 \times 2 \times 2 \times 5 \times 7$

2) A basket contains 20 balls and the average weight of each of these balls is $26\ g$. The five heaviest balls have an average weight of $40\ g$ each. If we remove the three heaviest balls from the basket, what is the average weight of the remaining balls?

   A. $10\ g$
   B. $21.33\ g$
   C. $30.78\ g$
   D. $35\ g$

3) How much greater is the value of $5x + 8$ than the value of $5x - 2$?

   A. 7
   B. 9
   C. 10
   D. 13

4) If 5 inches on a map represents an actual distance of 100 feet, then what actual distance does 16 inches on the map represent?

   A. 18 feet
   B. 100 feet
   C. 250 feet
   D. 320 feet

5) The circle graph below shows all Mr. Green's expenses for last month. If he spent $770 on his car, how much did he spend for his rent?

   A. $700
   B. $740
   C. $780
   D. $945

Mr. Green's monthly expenses

6) Alice drives from her house to work at an average speed of 52.5 miles per hour and she drives at an average speed of 60 miles per hour when she was returning home. What was her minimum speed on the round trip in miles per hour?

A. 55
B. 58.5
C. 42
D. Cannot be determined

7) The area of a circle is less than 81π. Which of the following can be the circumference of the circle?

A. $16\,\pi$
B. $18\,\pi$
C. $126\,\pi$
D. $32\,\pi$

8) Oscar purchased a new hat that was on sale for $7.38. The original price was $12.65. What percentage discount was the sale price?

A. 4.2%
B. 40.5%
C. 42%
D. 45%

9) If $f(x) = x^2 + 4$, what is the smallest possible value of $f(x)$?

A. 0
B. 4
C. 5
D. 7

10) If the sum of the positive integers from 1 to n is 2,350, and the sum of the positive integers from $n + 1$ to $2n$ is 4,356, which of the following represents the sum of the positive integers from 1 to $2n$ inclusive?

A. 2,106
B. 4,356
C. 6,000
D. 6,706

11) Which of the following statements is correct, according to the graph below?

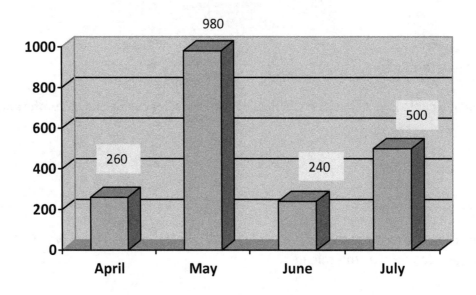

Number of Books Sold in a Bookstore

A. Number of books sold in April was twice the number of books sold in July.
B. Number of books sold in July was less than half the number of books sold in May.
C. Number of books sold in June was half the number of books sold in April.
D. Number of books sold in July was equal to the number of books sold in April and June.

12) List A consists of the numbers $\{2, 3, 8, 10, 18\}$, and list B consists of the numbers $\{5, 6, 12, 14, 20\}$.
    If the two lists are combined, what is the median of the combined list?

A. 6
B. 7
C. 8
D. 9

13) If Jim adds 120 stamps to his current stamp collection, the total number of stamps will be equal to $\frac{5}{4}$ the current number of stamps. If Jim adds 60% more stamps to the current collection, how many stamps will be in the collection?

A. 395
B. 550
C. 768
D. 950

14) A bag contains 18 balls: two green, five black, eight blue, a brown, a red and one white. If 11 balls are removed from the bag at random, what is the probability that a brown ball has been removed?

A. $\frac{1}{9}$

B. $\frac{1}{6}$

C. $\frac{16}{11}$

D. $\frac{11}{18}$

15) If $x + y = 7$ and $x - y = 5$ then what is the value of $(x^2 - y^2)$?

A. 23
B. 35
C. 65
D. 90

16) What's The ratio of boys and girls in a class is $3:8$. If there are 44 students in the class, how many more boys should be enrolled to make the ratio $1:1$?

A. 8
B. 10
C. 20
D. 22

17) The area of rectangle $ABCD$ is 245 square inches. If the length of the rectangle is five times the width, what is the perimeter of rectangle $ABCD$?

A. 68 inches
B. 84 inches
C. 102 inches
D. 126 inches

18) The sum of 8 numbers is greater than 240 and less than 320. Which of the following could be the average (arithmetic mean) of the numbers?

A. 30
B. 35
C. 40
D. 45

19) Which of the following expressions gives the value of n in terms of a, c, and z from the following equation?

$$a = [\frac{cz}{n}]^2$$

A. $n = ac^2z^2$

B. $n = \frac{cz}{\sqrt{a}}$

C. $n = \frac{\sqrt{a}}{cz}$

D. $n = [\frac{cz}{a}]^2$

20) Triangle ABC is similar to triangle ADE. What is the length of side EC?

A. 4

B. 7

C. 12

D. 14

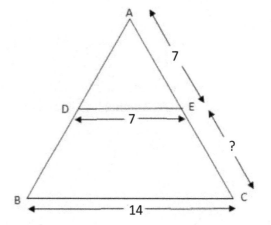

21) A gas tank can hold 20 gallons when it is $\frac{2}{5}$ full. How many gallons does it contain when it is full?

A. 125

B. 62.5

C. 50

D. 10

22)

Column A | Column B
The average of $12, 24,$ and 28 | The average of $16, 20,$ and 25

A. Quantity A is greater.
B. Quantity B is greater
C. The two quantities are equal.
D. The relationship cannot be determined from the information given.

23)

Column A | Column B
$13 \times 756 \times 17$ | $15 \times 756 \times 14$

A. Quantity A is greater.
B. Quantity B is greater
C. The two quantities are equal.
D. The relationship cannot be determined from the information given.

24) x is an integer

Column A | Column B
x | $\dfrac{x}{-3}$

A. Quantity A is greater.
B. Quantity B is greater
C. The two quantities are equal.
D. The relationship cannot be determined from the information given.

25)

Column A | Column B
The greatest value of x in $5|4x - 3| = 10$ | The greatest value of x in $5|4x + 3| = 10$

A. Quantity A is greater.
B. Quantity B is greater
C. The two quantities are equal.
D. The relationship cannot be determined from the information given.

26) x is an integer

Column A	Column B
$(x)^2(x)^3$	$(x^2)^3$

A. Quantity A is greater.
B. Quantity B is greater
C. The two quantities are equal.
D. The relationship cannot be determined from the information given.

27) Town A is 15 kilometers due north of Town B and Town C is 8 kilometers due west of Town B.

Column A	Column B
The shortest distance between Town C and Town A	17.5 miles

A. Quantity A is greater.
B. Quantity B is greater
C. The two quantities are equal.
D. The relationship cannot be determined from the information given.

28)

Column A	Column B
2^2	$\sqrt[4]{81}$

A. Quantity A is greater.
B. Quantity B is greater
C. The two quantities are equal.
D. The relationship cannot be determined from the information given.

29)

Column A	Column B
6	$(33)^{\frac{1}{2}}$

A. Quantity A is greater.
B. Quantity B is greater
C. The two quantities are equal.
D. The relationship cannot be determined from the information given.

30) The selling price of a sport jacket including 18% discount is $41.

     Column A   Column B
     Original price of the sport jacket $51

A. Quantity A is greater.
B. Quantity B is greater
C. The two quantities are equal.
D. The relationship cannot be determined from the information given.

31) Jessica has to do research for her PHD. The research report she needs to read costs $10.00. however, she can copy the x pages of the report that she really needs for $0.20 per page.

     Column A   Column B
     The greatest possible value of x, if the   50
     cost of copying the x pages is less than
     the cost of purchasing the whole
     report.

A. Quantity A is greater.
B. Quantity B is greater
C. The two quantities are equal.
D. The relationship cannot be determined from the information given.

32)
     Column A   Column B
     The probability of rolling a 6 on a die   The probability of rolling an even
     and getting heads on a coin toss.   number on a die and picking a spade
                                            from a deck of 52 cards.

A. Quantity A is greater.
B. Quantity B is greater
C. The two quantities are equal.
D. The relationship cannot be determined from the information given.

33)

Column A	Column B
$\left(\dfrac{1}{4}\right)^2$	4^{-2}

A. Quantity A is greater.
B. Quantity B is greater
C. The two quantities are equal.
D. The relationship cannot be determined from the information given.

34) Liza has a piano store, and she makes a profit of $315 on each sale of a piano and each piano costs her $1350.

Column A	Column B
The profit expressed as a percent of the cost to Liza.	The profit expressed as a percent of the sale price.

A. Quantity A is greater.
B. Quantity B is greater
C. The two quantities are equal.
D. The relationship cannot be determined from the information given.

35) $\dfrac{x}{y} = \dfrac{3}{5}$

Column A	Column B
$\dfrac{x}{y}$	$\dfrac{x+3}{y+5}$

A. Quantity A is greater.
B. Quantity B is greater
C. The two quantities are equal.
D. The relationship cannot be determined from the information given.

36) Ina certain numbers game, x is an odd integer, and y is an even integer. An odd number is considered greater than an even number. Below are two players' results.

Column A	Column B
$(x - y)^2 + x$	$(y)(x + y)$

A. Quantity A is greater.
B. Quantity B is greater
C. The two quantities are equal.
D. The relationship cannot be determined from the information given.

37) $x^2 - 4x - 15 = 6$

Column A	Column B
x	0

A. Quantity A is greater.
B. Quantity B is greater
C. The two quantities are equal.
D. The relationship cannot be determined from the information given.

IF YOU FINISH BEFORE TIME IS CALLED, YOU MAY CHECK YOUR WORK ON THIS SECTION.

STOP

ISEE Upper Level

Practice Test 5

Part 2 (Mathematics Achievement)

- o **47 questions**

- o **Total time for this section: 40** Minutes

- o **Calculators are not allowed at the test.**

1) $\dfrac{1}{7b^2} + \dfrac{1}{7b} = \dfrac{1}{b^2}$, then $b = ?$

A. $-\dfrac{16}{15}$

B. 6

C. $-\dfrac{15}{16}$

D. 8

2) $\dfrac{|3+x|}{7} \le 8$, then $= ?$

A. $-38 \le x \le 53$
B. $-59 \le x \le 53$
C. $-59 \le x \le 38$
D. $-32 \le x \le 32$

3) The cost, in thousands of dollars, of producing x thousands of textbooks is $C(x) = x^2 + 2x$. The revenue, also in thousands of dollars, is $R(x) = 40x$. find the profit or loss if 10 textbooks are produced. $(profit = revenue - cost)$

A. $\$2,160 \ profit$
B. $\$280 \ profit$
C. $\$2,160 \ loss$
D. $\$280 \ loss$

4) Ella (E) is 7 years older than her friend Ava (A) who is 3 years younger than her sister Sofia (S). If E, A and S denote their ages, which one of the following represents the given information?

A. $\begin{cases} E = A + 7 \\ S = A - 3 \end{cases}$

B. $\begin{cases} E = A + 7 \\ A = S + 3 \end{cases}$

C. $\begin{cases} A = E + 7 \\ S = A - 3 \end{cases}$

D. $\begin{cases} E = A + 7 \\ A = S - 3 \end{cases}$

5) 5 less than twice a positive integer is 73. What is the integer?
A. 39
B. 41
C. 42
D. 44

6) Which of the following points lies on the line $4x + 6y = 20$?
A. $(2,1)$
B. $(-1,3)$
C. $(-3,4)$
D. $(2,2)$

7) An angle is equal to one fourth of its supplement. What is the measure of that angle?
A. $20°$
B. $36°$
C. $45°$
D. $60°$

8) 1.2 is what percent of 15?
A. 1.2
B. 8
C. 15
D. 24

9) Right triangle ABC has two legs of lengths $5 \, cm$ (AB) and $12 \, cm$ (AC). What is the length of the third side (BC)?
A. $4 \, cm$
B. $6 \, cm$
C. $8 \, cm$
D. $13 \, cm$

10) Simplify $8x^2y^3(2x^2y)^3 =$
A. $12x^4y^6$
B. $12x^8y^6$
C. $64x^4y^6$
D. $64x^8y^6$

11) Which is the longest time?

A. $22 \, hours$
B. $1,520 \, minutes$
C. $2 \, days$
D. $5,200 \, seconds$

12) Write 515 in expanded form, using exponents.

A. $(5 \times 10^3) + (2 \times 10^2) + (3 \times 10)$
B. $(5 \times 10^2) + (2 \times 10^1) - 5$
C. $(5 \times 10^2) + (2 \times 10^1) + 3$
D. $(5 \times 10^1) + (2 \times 10^2) + 3$

13) A company pays its writer $4 for every 400 words written. How much will a writer earn for an article with 860 words?

A. $11
B. $5.6
C. $8.6
D. $9.6

14) A circular logo is enlarged to fit the lid of a jar. The new diameter is 40% larger than the original. By what percentage has the area of the logo increased?

A. 20%
B. 30%
C. 69%
D. 96%

15) A circle has a diameter of 12 inches. What is its approximate circumference?

A. 6.28 inches
B. 25.12 inches
C. 34.85 inches
D. 37.68 inches

16) What is the area of an isosceles right triangle that has one leg that measures $8 \ cm$?

A. $32 \ cm^2$
B. $64 \ cm^2$
C. $6\sqrt{2} \ cm^2$
D. $72 \ cm^2$

17) What's the area of the non-shaded part of the following figure?

A. 192
B. 176
C. 40
D. 42

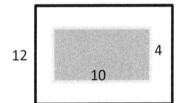

18) $79.22 \div 0.04 \ = ?$

A. 19.805
B. 1,980.5
C. 1,98.05
D. 1.9805

19) A bread recipe calls for $2\frac{2}{3}$ cups of flour. If you only have $1\frac{5}{6}$ cups, how much more flour is needed?

A. 1

B. $\frac{1}{2}$

C. 2

D. $\frac{5}{6}$

20) The equation of a line is given as : $y = 5x - 3$. Which of the following points does not lie on the line?

A. $(1, 2)$
B. $(-2, -13)$
C. $(3, 12)$
D. $(2, 8)$

21) The drivers at a trucking company must report the mileage on their trucks each week. The mileage reading of Ed's vehicle was 39,750 at the beginning of one week, and 40,128 at the end of the same week. What was the total number of miles driven by Ed that week?

A. 218 *miles*
B. 378 *miles*
C. 410 *miles*
D. 505 *miles*

22) Which equation represents the statement "three plus the sum of the squares of w and x is 35"?

A. $3 + (w^2 + x) = 35$
B. $3(w^2 + x) = 35$
C. $(w^2 + x) - 3 = 35$
D. $\frac{(w^2 + x)}{3} = 35$

23) What is the solution of the following system of equations?
$$\begin{cases} -2x - y = -9 \\ -5x - 2y = 18 \end{cases}$$

A. $(-1, 2)$
B. $(-36, 81)$
C. $(36, 81)$
D. $(4, -2)$

24) What is the area of an isosceles right triangle that has one leg that measures $5\ cm$?

A. $12.5\ cm^2$
B. $25\ cm^2$
C. $6\sqrt{2}\ cm^2$
D. $72\ cm^2$

25) Which of the following is a factor of both $x^2 - 2x - 8$ and $x^2 + 6x + 8$?

A. $(x - 4)$
B. $(x + 4)$
C. $(x - 2)$
D. $(x + 2)$

26) $\dfrac{12}{25}$ is equal to:

A. 4.8
B. 0.48
C. 0.04
D. 0.4

27) If $x + y = 13$, what is the value of $8x + 8y$?

A. 192
B. 48
C. 85
D. 104

28) $\begin{array}{r} 37\text{ hr. }25\text{ min.} \\ -\ 23\text{ hr. }38\text{ min.} \\ \hline \end{array}$

A. $12\ hr.\,57\ min.$
B. $12\ hr.\,47\ min.$
C. $13\ hr.\,47\ min.$
D. $13\ hr.\,57\ min.$

29) A car uses 18 gallons of gas to travel 450 miles. How many miles per gallon does the car get?

A. $25\ miles\ per\ gallon$
B. $32\ miles\ per\ gallon$
C. $30\ miles\ per\ gallon$
D. $34\ miles\ per\ gallon$

30) Find the perimeter of a rectangle with the dimensions 89×55.

A. 4,895

B. 288

C. 144

D. 134

31) What's the reciprocal of $\frac{x^3}{12}$?

A. $\frac{12}{x^3} - 1$

B. $\frac{48}{x^3}$

C. $\frac{12}{x^3} + 1$

D. $\frac{12}{x^3}$

32) Mario loaned Jett $1,300 at a yearly interest rate of 5%. After one year what is the interest owned on this loan?

A. $1,260

B. $120

C. $65

D. $30

33) Ellis just got hired for on-the-road sales and will travel about 2,900 miles a week during an 80-hour work week. If the time spent traveling is $\frac{3}{5}$ of his week, how many hours a week will he be on the road?

A. Ellis spends about 34 hours of his 80-hour work week on the road.

B. Ellis spends about 40 hours of his 80-hour work week on the road.

C. Ellis spends about 43 hours of his 80-hour work week on the road.

D. Ellis spends about 48 hours of his 80-hour work week on the road.

34) Given that $x = 0.6$ and $y = 6$, what is the value of $2x^2(y + 5)$?

A. 7.92

B. 8.2

C. 12.2

D. 13.2

35) Karen is 9 years older than her sister Michelle, and Michelle is 4 years younger than her brother David. If the sum of their ages is 85, how old is Michelle?

A. 21
B. 25
C. 29
D. 24

36) Calculate the area of a parallelogram with a base of 2 feet and height of 2.8 feet.

A. $2.8\ square\ feet$
B. $5.2\ square\ feet$
C. $5.6\ square\ feet$
D. $5.0\ square\ feet$

37) A shirt costing $200 is discounted 15%. After a month, the shirt is discounted another 15%. Which of the following expressions can be used to find the selling price of the shirt?

A. $(200)\,(0.70)$
B. $(200) - 200\,(0.30)$
C. $(200)(0.15) - (200)\,(0.15)$
D. $(200)\,(0.85)\,(0.85)$

38) In a school, the ratio of number of boys to girls is 3: 7. If the number of boys is 150, what is the total number of students in the school?

A. 390
B. 500
C. 540
D. 600

39) A tree 32 feet tall casts a shadow 15 feet long. Jack is 6 feet tall. How long is Jack's shadow?

A. $2.81\ ft$
B. $4\ ft$
C. $4.25\ ft$
D. $8\ ft$

40) What is the area of the shaded region if the diameter of the bigger circle is 12 inches and the diameter of the smaller circle is 6 inches.

A. $16\ \pi\ inch^2$
B. $27\ \pi\ inch^2$
C. $36\ \pi inch^2$
D. $80\ \pi inch^2$

41) What is the result of the expression?

$$\begin{vmatrix} 4 & 6 \\ -1 & -7 \\ -5 & -1 \end{vmatrix} + \begin{vmatrix} 0 & -1 \\ 6 & 0 \\ 2 & 3 \end{vmatrix} ?$$

A. $\begin{vmatrix} 0 & -1 \\ 7 & 0 \\ 2 & 3 \end{vmatrix}$

B. $\begin{vmatrix} 4 & 6 \\ -1 & -3 \\ -5 & -1 \end{vmatrix}$

C. $\begin{vmatrix} 4 & 5 \\ 5 & -7 \\ -3 & 2 \end{vmatrix}$

D. $\begin{vmatrix} 0 & -3 \\ -7 & 0 \\ -10 & -3 \end{vmatrix}$

42) How many square feet of tile is needed for a 17 foot × 17 foot room?

A. 72 *square feet*
B. 108 *square feet*
C. 289 *square feet*
D. 216 *square feet*

43) $(3x + 4)(x + 5) =$

A. $4x + 8$
B. $3x + 3x + 20$
C. $3x^2 + 19x + 20$
D. $3x^2 + 3$

44) If $x \blacksquare y = \sqrt{x^2 + y}$, what is the value of $7 \blacksquare 15$?

A. $\sqrt{126}$
B. 8
C. 4
D. 3

45) There are three equal tanks of water. If $\frac{2}{5}$ of a tank contains 150 liters of water, what is the capacity of the three tanks of water together?

A. 1,125 liters
B. 500 liters
C. 240 liters
D. 80 liters

46) The average weight of 18 girls in a class is $50\ kg$ and the average weight of 32 boys in the same class is $62\ kg$. What is the average weight of all the 50 students in that class?

A. $50\ kg$
B. $57.68\ kg$
C. $61.68\ kg$
D. $61.9\ kg$

47) If x is 45% percent of 720, what is x?

A. 185
B. 324
C. 402
D. 720

IF YOU FINISH BEFORE TIME IS CALLED, YOU MAY CHECK YOUR WORK ON THIS SECTION.   STOP

ISEE Upper Level Practice Tests
Answer Keys

Now, it's time to review your results to see where you went wrong and what areas you need to improve!

ISEE Upper Level Math Practice Test 1 Answer Key							
Quantitative Reasoning				Mathematics Achievement			
1	C	17	A	33	D	1	B	17	A	33	B
2	C	18	D	34	D	2	D	18	B	34	A
3	C	19	B	35	A	3	D	19	D	35	C
4	A	20	C	36	B	4	C	20	C	36	C
5	A	21	B	37	B	5	A	21	D	37	D
6	B	22	B			6	B	22	B	38	D
7	C	23	C			7	B	23	A	39	D
8	B	24	A			8	D	24	B	40	D
9	B	25	B			9	B	25	D	41	D
10	A	26	A			10	A	26	B	42	B
11	D	27	C			11	B	27	D	43	B
12	A	28	A			12	C	28	A	44	A
13	A	29	A			13	D	29	D	45	C
14	A	30	A			14	A	30	B	46	D
15	A	31	D			15	D	31	A	47	C
16	D	32	A			16	C	32	D		

ISEE Upper Level Math Practice Test 2 Answer Key

Quantitative Reasoning

1	B	17	B	33	C			
2	B	18	B	34	A			
3	C	19	B	35	A			
4	D	20	B	36	A			
5	D	21	B	37	D			
6	D	22	A					
7	A	23	B					
8	C	24	D					
9	C	25	A					
10	D	26	D					
11	C	27	D					
12	C	28	C					
13	D	29	A					
14	D	30	A					
15	B	31	B					
16	C	32	B					

Mathematics Achievement

1	B	17	B	33	D			
2	B	18	B	34	A			
3	B	19	B	35	B			
4	D	20	C	36	C			
5	D	21	C	37	D			
6	A	22	D	38	D			
7	B	23	B	39	A			
8	B	24	A	40	B			
9	D	25	A	41	C			
10	D	26	B	42	C			
11	C	27	C	43	C			
12	C	28	B	44	B			
13	C	29	C	45	A			
14	C	30	C	46	B			
15	B	31	D	47	B			
16	A	32	C					

ISEE Upper Level Math Practice Test 3 Answer Key

Quantitative Reasoning						Mathematics Achievement					
1	D	17	D	33	A	1	A	17	B	33	B
2	C	18	B	34	B	2	A	18	B	34	C
3	B	19	A	35	A	3	A	19	C	35	B
4	B	20	A	36	B	4	B	20	C	36	D
5	C	21	B	37	A	5	D	21	D	37	C
6	B	22	D			6	C	22	B	38	D
7	C	23	C			7	D	23	B	39	C
8	B	24	B			8	A	24	A	40	D
9	A	25	D			9	B	25	B	41	D
10	B	26	D			10	D	26	C	42	D
11	A	27	B			11	B	27	B	43	A
12	C	28	A			12	A	28	D	44	B
13	D	29	A			13	C	29	C	45	B
14	B	30	C			14	D	30	A	46	D
15	A	31	D			15	B	31	A	47	D
16	A	32	D			16	A	32	C		

ISEE Upper Level Math Practice Test 4 Answer Key

Quantitative Reasoning

1	C	17	D	33	D
2	B	18	D	34	B
3	D	19	D	35	B
4	A	20	B	36	A
5	A	21	B	37	A
6	C	22	A		
7	C	23	B		
8	D	24	A		
9	D	25	B		
10	C	26	D		
11	C	27	C		
12	D	28	A		
13	D	29	A		
14	D	30	D		
15	B	31	D		
16	A	32	A		

Mathematics Achievement

1	D	17	B	33	C
2	D	18	A	34	D
3	A	19	D	35	D
4	B	20	D	36	A
5	A	21	B	37	B
6	B	22	C	38	D
7	B	23	C	39	A
8	C	24	A	40	A
9	D	25	A	41	B
10	A	26	C	42	C
11	C	27	B	43	C
12	C	28	C	44	C
13	C	29	C	45	A
14	B	30	A	46	C
15	C	31	D	47	C
16	B	32	B		

ISEE Upper Level Math Practice Test 5 Answer Key

Quantitative Reasoning								Mathematics Achievement							

1	D	17	B	33	C	1	B	17	B	33	D
2	B	18	B	34	A	2	B	18	B	34	A
3	C	19	B	35	C	3	B	19	D	35	D
4	D	20	B	36	C	4	D	20	D	36	C
5	D	21	C	37	D	5	A	21	B	37	D
6	D	22	A			6	D	22	A	38	B
7	A	23	A			7	B	23	B	39	A
8	C	24	D			8	B	24	A	40	B
9	B	25	A			9	D	25	D	41	C
10	D	26	D			10	D	26	B	42	C
11	D	27	B			11	C	27	D	43	C
12	D	28	A			12	B	28	C	44	B
13	C	29	A			13	C	29	A	45	A
14	D	30	B			14	D	30	B	46	B
15	B	31	B			15	D	31	D	47	B
16	C	32	B			16	A	32	C		

Score Your Test

ISEE scores are broken down by four sections: Verbal Reasoning, Reading Comprehension, Quantitative Reasoning, and Mathematics Achievement. A sum of the ALL sections is also reported. The Essay section is scored separately.

For the Upper Level ISEE, the score range is 760 to 940, the lowest possible score a student can earn is 760 and the highest score is 940 for each section. A student receives 1 point for every correct answer. There is no penalty for wrong or skipped questions.

The total scaled score for an Upper Level ISEE test is the sum of the scores for all sections. A student will also receive a percentile score of between 1-99% that compares that student's test scores with those of other test takers of same grade and gender from the past 3 years. When a student receives her/his score, the percentile score is also be broken down into a stanine and the stanines are ranging from 1–9. Most schools accept students with scores of 5–9. The ideal candidate has scores of 6 or higher.

Percentile Rank	Stanine
1 – 3	1
4 – 10	2
11- 22	3
23 - 39	4
40 – 59	5
60 – 76	6
77- 88	7
89 – 95	8
96 - 99	9

The following charts provide an estimate of students ISEE percentile rankings for the practice tests, compared against other students taking these tests. Keep in mind that these percentiles are estimates only, and your actual ISEE percentile will depend on the specific group of students taking the exam in your year.

ISEE Upper Level Quantitative Reasoning Percentiles			
Grade Applying to	25th Percentile	50th Percentile	75th Percentile
9th	850	880	895
10th	855	885	900
11th	860	890	905
12th	864	892	908

Use the next table to convert ISEE Upper level raw score to scaled score for application to 9th - 12th grade.

ISEE Upper Level Scaled Scores									
Raw Score	Quantitative Reasoning		Mathematics Achievement		Raw Score	Quantitative Reasoning		Mathematics Achievement	
	Report Range		Report Range			Report Range		Report Range	
0	760	760	760	760	26	900	885	885	865
1	770	765	770	765	27	905	890	885	865
2	780	770	780	770	28	910	895	890	870
3	790	775	790	775	29	910	900	890	870
4	800	780	800	780	30	915	905	895	875
5	810	785	810	785	31	920	910	895	875
6	820	790	820	790	32	925	915	900	880
7	825	795	825	795	33	930	920	900	880
8	830	800	830	800	34	930	925	905	885
9	835	805	835	805	35	935	930	905	885
10	840	810	840	810	36	935	935	910	890
11	845	815	845	815	37	940	940	910	890
12	850	820	850	820	38			915	895
13	855	825	855	825	39			920	900
14	860	830	855	830	40			925	905
15	865	835	860	835	41			925	910
16	870	840	860	840	42			930	915
17	875	845	865	840	43			930	920
18	880	845	865	845	44			935	925
19	880	850	870	845	45			935	930
20	885	855	870	850	46			940	935
21	885	860	875	850	47			940	940
22	890	865	875	855					
23	890	870	875	855					
24	895	875	880	860					
25	895	880	880	860					

ISEE Upper Level Practice Tests
Answers and Explanations

ISEE Upper Level Practice Test 1
Quantitative Reasoning

1) Choice C is correct

The diagonal of the square is 4. Let x be the side.
Use Pythagorean Theorem: $a^2 + b^2 = c^2$
$x^2 + x^2 = 4^2 \Rightarrow 2x^2 = 4^2 \Rightarrow 2x^2 = 16 \Rightarrow x^2 = 8 \Rightarrow x = \sqrt{8}$
The area of the square is: $\sqrt{8} \times \sqrt{8} = 8$

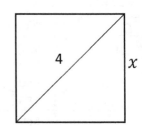

2) Choice C is correct

$$Probability = \frac{number\ of\ desired\ outcomes}{number\ of\ total\ outcomes}$$
In this case, a desired outcome is selecting either a red or a yellow marble. Combine the number of red and yellow marbles: $8 + 5 = 13$, and divide this by the total number of marbles: $6 + 8 + 5 = 19$. The probability is. $\frac{13}{19}$

3) Choice C is correct

A factor must divide evenly into its multiple. 14 cannot be a factor of 80 because 80 divided by $14 = 5.71$

4) Choice A is correct

To find what percent A is of B, divide A by B, then multiply that number by 100%:
$12.25 \div 68.65 = 0.1784 \times 100\% = 17.84\%$,   This is approximately 18%.

5) Choice A is correct

The total cost of the phone call can be represented by the equation: $TC = \$4.00 + \$0.4x$, where x is the duration of the call after the first five minutes. In this case, $x = 30$. Substitute the known values into the equation and solve: $TC = \$4.00 + \$0.4 \times 30$
$TC = \$4.00 + \$12.00$, $TC = \$16.00$

6) Choice B is correct

Let b be the amount of time Alec can do the job, then,

$$\frac{1}{a} + \frac{1}{b} = \frac{1}{100} \rightarrow \frac{1}{300} + \frac{1}{b} = \frac{1}{100} \rightarrow \frac{1}{b} = \frac{1}{100} - \frac{1}{300} = \frac{2}{300} = \frac{1}{150}$$

Then: $b = 150$ minutes

7) Choice C is correct

Begin by calculating James's total earnings after 30 hours: $30 \ hours \times \$7.500 \ per \ hour = \$225$. Next, divide this total by Jacob's hourly rate to find the number of hours Jacob would need to work: $\$225 \div \$9.00 \ per \ hour = 25 \ hours$

8) Choice B is correct
The distance on the map is proportional to the actual distance between the two cities. Use the information to set up a proportion and then solve for the unknown number of actual miles: $\frac{12 \ miles}{\frac{1}{3} \ inch} = \frac{x \ miles}{20 \ inche}$, Cross multiply and simplify to solve for the x:

$$\frac{12 \times 20}{\frac{1}{3}} = x \ miles \rightarrow \frac{240}{\frac{1}{3}} = 240 \times 3 = 720 \ miles$$

9) Choice B is correct
Number of Mathematics book: $0.30 \times 840 = 252$, Number of English books: $0.15 \times 840 = 126$, Product of number of Mathematics and number of English books: $252 \times 126 = 31,752$

10) Choice A is correct

First, find the number. Let x be the number. Write the equation and solve for x. 150% of a number is 75, then: $1.5 \times x = 75 \rightarrow x = 75 \div 1.5 = 50$, 80% of 50 is: $0.8 \times 50 = 40$

11) Choice D is correct

$3y + 5 < 29 \rightarrow 3y < 29 - 5 \rightarrow 3y < 24 \rightarrow y < 8$. Only choice D (2.5) is less than 8.

12) Choice A is correct

The length of MN is equal to: $3x + 5x = 8x$, Then: $8x = 40 \rightarrow x = \frac{40}{8} = 5$
The length of ON is equal to: $5x = 5 \times 5 = 25 \ cm$

13) Choice A is correct
Begin by examining the sequence to find the pattern. The difference between 2 and 5 is 3; moving from 5 to 10 requires 5 to be added; moving from 10 to 17 requires 7 to be added. The pattern emerges here — adding by consecutive odd integers. The 5th term is equal to $17 + 9 = 26$, and the 6th term is equal to $26 + 11 = 37$.

14) Choice A is correct

Write equations based on the information provided in the question:
$Emily = Daniel, \quad Emily = 5 \ Claire, \quad Daniel = 16 + Claire$
$Emily = Daniel \quad \rightarrow \quad Emily = 16 + Claire$
$Emily = 5 \ Claire \rightarrow \quad 5 \ Claire = 16 + Claire \quad \rightarrow \quad 5 \ Claire - Claire = 16$
$4 \ Claire = 16, Claire = 4$

15) Choice A is correct

The general slope-intercept form of the equation of a line is $y = mx + b$, where m is the slope and b is the y-intercept. By substitution of the given point and given slope: $-2 = (7)(2) + b$, So, $b = -2 - 14 = -16$, and the required equation is $y = 7x - 16$.

16) Choice D is correct

If each book weighs $\frac{1}{5}$ pound, then $1\ pound = 5\ books$. To find the number of books in 50 pounds, simply multiply this 5 by 50: $50 \times 5 = 250$

17) Choice A is correct

Let's choose $100 for the sales of the supermarket. If the sales increases by 10 percent in April, the final amount of sales at the end of April will be $100 + (10\%) \times (\$100) = \$110$.
If sales then decreased by 10 percent in May, the final amount of sales at the end of August will be $\$110 - (\$110) \times (10\%) = \$99$. The final sales of $99 is 99% of the original price of $100. Therefore, the sales decreased by 1% overall.

18) Choice D is correct

Multiplying each side of $-3x - y = 6$ by 2 gives $-6x - 2y = 12$. Adding each side of $-6x - 2y = 12$ to the corresponding side of $6x + 4y = 10$ gives $2y = 22$ or $y = 11$. Finally, substituting 11 for y in $6x + 4y = 10$ gives $6x + 4(11) = 10$ or $x = -\frac{17}{3}$.

19) Choice B is correct

The time it takes to drive from city A to city B is: $\frac{2600}{68} = 38.23$ hours

20) Choice C is correct

Let x be the number. Write the equation and solve for x. $\frac{2}{3} \times 18 = \frac{2}{5}x \rightarrow \frac{2 \times 18}{3} = \frac{2x}{5}$, use cross multiplication to solve for x. $5 \times 36 = 2x \times 3 \Rightarrow 180 = 6x \Rightarrow x = 30$

21) Choice B is correct

The question is this: 530.40 is what percent of 624? Use percent formula: $Part = \frac{percent}{100} \times whole$,
$530.40 = \frac{percent}{100} \times 624 \rightarrow 530.40 = \frac{percent \times 624}{100} \rightarrow 53040 = percent \times 624$
Then, Percent $= \frac{53040}{624} = 85$, 530.40 is 85% of 624. Therefore, the discount is: $100\% - 85\% = 15\%$

22) Choice B is correct

Column A: $5\% = \frac{5}{100} = 0.05$,   Column B: $\frac{1}{2} = 0.5$,   0.5 is greater than 0.05

23) Choice C is correct

Recall that the first and only even prime number is 2. The other prime numbers are: $3, 5, 7, 9, 11, 13, 17$, etc. They are all odd numbers except for 2, so the sum of members in Set A is just 2. So, the correct answer is C.

24) Choice A is correct

The posts are placed 12.5 feet apart. Since a post is needed at the very beginning as well as at the end, A requires 9 posts. $100 \div 12.5 = 8, \quad 8 + 1 = 9$

25) Choice B is correct

Column A: $\frac{12 + 18 + 26 + 30 + 32}{5} = \frac{118}{5} = 23.6$, Column B: $\frac{24 + 28 + 30 + 36}{4} = \frac{118}{4} = 29.5$

26) Choice A is correct

Column A: $9 + 12(9 - 5) = 57$, Column B: $12 + 9(9 - 5) = 48$

27) Choice C is correct

First find the value of x. $\frac{x}{48} = \frac{2}{3} \rightarrow 3x = 2 \times 48 = 96 \rightarrow x = \frac{96}{3} = 32$

Column A: $\frac{8}{x} = \frac{8}{32} = \frac{1}{4}$

28) Choice A is correct

First convert hours to minutes. 2 hours 5 $minutes = 2 \times 60 + 5 = 125$ $minutes$.
Machine D makes b rolls of steel in 25 minutes. So, it makes 5 sets of b in 125 minutes. $125 \div 25 = 5$ sets of b. Machine E operates for 4 hours, making b rolls per hour. So, it makes a total of $4b$ rolls. Therefore, machine D makes more rolls, and Column A is greater.

29) Choice A is correct

The ratio of boys to girls in a class is 7 to 11. Therefore, ratio of boys to the entire class is 7 out of 18. $\frac{7}{18} > \frac{1}{3}$

30) Choice A is correct

Let us calculate each probability individually:
That probability that the first marble is blue = $\frac{6}{10} = \frac{3}{5}$
The probability that the second marble is blue = $\frac{5}{9}$
Column A: The probability that both marbles are blue = $\frac{3}{5} \times \frac{5}{9} = \frac{15}{45} = \frac{1}{3}$
The probability that the marble is green = $\frac{4}{10} = \frac{2}{5}$
The probability that the second marble is blue = $\frac{6}{9} = \frac{2}{3}$

Column B: The probability that the first marbles is green, but the second is blue = $\frac{2}{5} \times \frac{2}{3} = \frac{4}{15}$

Column A is greater. $\frac{1}{3} > \frac{4}{15}$.

31) Choice D is correct

First, solve the expression for x. $\frac{x}{4} = y^2 \rightarrow x = 4y^2$. Plug in different values for y and find the values of x. Let's choose $y = 0 \rightarrow x = 4y^2 \rightarrow x = 4(0)^2 = 0$. The values in Column A and B are equal. Now, let's choose $y = 1 \rightarrow x = 4y^2 \rightarrow x = 4(1)^2 = 4$. Column A is greater. So, the relationship cannot be determined from the information given.

32) Choice A is correct

Column A: $3x^2 - 2x + 4 = 3(-1)^2 - 2(-1) + 4 = 3 + 2 + 4 = 9$
Column B: $2x^3 + x^2 + 4 = 2(-1)^3 + (-1)^2 + 4 = -2 + 1 + 4 = 3$

33) Choice D is correct

$6 > y > -2$,   Let's choose some values for y. $y = -1$
Column A: $\frac{y}{4} = \frac{-1}{4}$, Column B: $\frac{4}{y} = \frac{4}{-1} = -1$, In this case, column A is bigger. $y = 1$
Column A: $\frac{y}{4} = \frac{1}{4}$, Column B: $\frac{4}{y} = \frac{4}{1} = 4$
In this case, Column B is bigger. So, the relationship cannot be determined from the information given.

34) Choice D is correct

$\frac{a}{b} = \frac{c}{d}$, Here there are two equal fractions. Let's choose some values for these variables. $\frac{1}{2} = \frac{2}{4}$,
In this case, Column A is 3 $(1 + 2)$ and Column B is 6 $(2 + 4)$. Since, we can change the positions of these variables (for example put 2 for a and 4 for b), he relationship cannot be determined from the information given.

35) Choice A is correct

First, let's find the number of digits when the printer prints 100 pages. If there are 2 digits in each page and the printer prints 100 pages, then, there will be 200 digits. $100 \times 2 = 200$. However, we know that pages $1 - 9$ have only one digit each, so we must subtract 9 from this total $200 - 9 = 191$. We also know that the number 100th has three digits not two. So, we must add 1 digit to this total: $191 + 1 = 192$. It is given that 195 digits were printed, and we know that 100 pages results in 192 digits total, so there must be 101 total pages in the magazine. Column A is greater.

36) Choice B is correct

Column A: The largest number that can be written by rearranging the digits in $263 = 632$
Column B: The largest number that can be written by rearranging the digits in $192 = 921$

37) Choice B is correct

The computer priced $124 includes 4% profit. Let x be the original cost of the computer. Then:
$x + 4\% \ of \ x = 124 \rightarrow x + 0.04x = 124 \rightarrow 1.04x = 124 \rightarrow x = \frac{124}{1.04} = 119.23$
Column B is bigger.

ISEE Upper Level Practice Test 1
Mathematics Achievement

1) Choice B is correct

Use quadratic formula: $ax^2 + bx + c = 0, x_{1,2} = \frac{-b \pm \sqrt{b^2 - 4ac}}{2a}$
$4x^2 + 14x + 6 = 0 \Rightarrow$ then: $a = 4, b = 14$ and $c = 6$
$x = \frac{-14 + \sqrt{14^2 - 4 \times 4 \times 6}}{2 \times 4} = -\frac{1}{2}, x = \frac{-14 - \sqrt{14^2 - 4 \times 4 \times 6}}{2 \times 4} = -3$

2) Choice D is correct

Use FOIL (First, Out, In, Last) method. $(x + 7)(x + 5) = x^2 + 5x + 7x + 35 = x^2 + 12x + 35$

3) Choice D is correct

Solve for x. $-4 \leq 4x - 8 < 16 \Rightarrow$ (add 8 all sides) $-4 + 8 \leq 4x - 8 + 8 < 16 + 8 \Rightarrow$
$4 \leq 4x < 24 \Rightarrow$ (divide all sides by 4) $1 \leq x < 6$. x is between 1 and 6. Choice D represent this inequality.

4) Choice C is correct

Simplify: $|9 - (12 \div |2 - 5|)| = |9 - (12 \div |-3|)| = |9 - (12 \div 3)| = |9 - 4| = |5| = 5$

5) Choice A is correct.

$0.00002389 = \frac{2.389}{100,000} \Rightarrow 2.389 \times 10^{-5}$

6) Choice B is correct.

A linear equation is a relationship between two variables, x and y, and can be written in the form of $y = mx + b$. A non-proportional linear relationship takes on the form $y = mx + b$, where $b \neq 0$ and its graph is a line that does not cross through the origin. Only in graph B, the line does not pass through the origin.

7) Choice B is correct.

Translated 5 units down and 4 units to the left means: $(x.y) \Rightarrow (x - 4, y - 5)$

8) Choice D is correct.

Write the proportion and solve for missing side.

$$\frac{\text{Smaller triangle height}}{\text{Smaller triangle base}} = \frac{\text{Bigger triangle height}}{\text{Bigger triangle base}} \Rightarrow \frac{90\,cm}{160\,cm} = \frac{90+\quad cm}{x} \Rightarrow x = 800\ cm$$

9) Choice B is correct.

$\frac{3}{22} = 0.136$ and $19\% = 0.19$ therefore x should be between 0.136 and 0.19

Only choice B ($\frac{5}{36} = 0.138$) is between 0.136 and 0.19

10) Choice A is correct

The ratio of boy to girls is $2:3$. Therefore, there are 2 boys out of 5 students. To find the answer, first divide the total number of students by 5, then multiply the result by 2.
$600 \div 5 = 120 \Rightarrow 120 \times 2 = 240$

11) Choice B is correct

Simplify: $2 - 10 \div (4^2 \div 2) = 2 - 10 \div (16 \div 2) = \frac{3}{4}$

12) Choice C is correct

All Integers must end in one of the following digits:
0 when multiplied by itself ends in 0,1 when multiplied by itself ends in 1,2 when multiplied by itself ends in 4,3 when multiplied by itself ends in 9,4 when multiplied by itself ends in 6,5 when multiplied by itself ends in 5,6 when multiplied by itself ends in 6,7 when multiplied by itself ends in 9,8 when multiplied by itself ends in 4,9 when multiplied by itself ends in 1 ,Number 8 is not in the results.

13) Choice D is correct

$\frac{1}{3}$ of the distance $5\frac{1}{4}$ miles is: $\frac{1}{3} \times 5\frac{1}{4} = \frac{1}{3} \times \frac{21}{4} = \frac{21}{12}$
Converting $\frac{21}{12}$ to a mixed number gives: $\frac{21}{12} = 1\frac{9}{12} = 1\frac{3}{4}$

14) Choice A is correct

Use Pythagorean theorem: $a^2 + b^2 = c^2 \rightarrow s^2 + h^2 = (5s)^2 \rightarrow s^2 + h^2 = 25s^2$
Subtracting s^2 from both sides gives: $h^2 = 24s^2$
Square roots of both sides: $h = \sqrt{24s^2} = \sqrt{4 \times 6 \times s^2} = \sqrt{4} \times \sqrt{6} \times \sqrt{s^2} = 2 \times s \times \sqrt{6} = 2s\sqrt{6}$

15) Choice D is correct

Let x be the number of purple marbles. Let's review the choices provided:

A. $\frac{1}{10}$, if the probability of choosing a purple marble is one out of ten, then:

$$Probability = \frac{number\ of\ desired\ outcomes}{number\ of\ total\ outcomes} = \frac{x}{20 + 30 + 40 + x} = \frac{1}{10}$$

Use cross multiplication and solve for x. $10x = 90 + x \rightarrow 9x = 90 \rightarrow x = 9$

Since, number of purple marbles can be 9, then, choice be the probability of randomly selecting a purple marble from the bag. Use same method for other choices.

B. $\frac{1}{4}$

$$\frac{x}{20 + 30 + 40 + x} = \frac{1}{4} \rightarrow 4x = 90 + x \rightarrow 3x = 90 \rightarrow x = 30$$

C. $\frac{2}{5}$

$$\frac{x}{20 + 30 + 40 + x} = \frac{2}{5} \rightarrow 5x = 180 + 2x \rightarrow 3x = 180 \rightarrow x = 60$$

D. $\frac{7}{15}$

$$\frac{x}{20 + 30 + 40 + x} = \frac{7}{15} \rightarrow 15x = 630 + 7x \rightarrow 8x = 630 \rightarrow x = 78.75$$

Number of purple marbles cannot be a decimal.

16) Choice C is correct

The area of the trapezoid is: $Area = \frac{1}{2}h(b_1 + b_2) = \frac{1}{2}(x)(13 + 8) = 126 \ cm^2$
$\rightarrow 10.5x = 126 \rightarrow x = 12 \ cm, y = \sqrt{5^2 + 12^2} = \sqrt{25 + 144} = \sqrt{169} = 13 \ cm$
The perimeter of the trapezoid is: $12 + 13 + 8 + 13 = 46 \ cm$

17) Choice A is correct

$$average = \frac{sum}{total} = \frac{32 + 35 + 29}{3} = \frac{96}{3} = 32 \ Miles$$

18) Choice B is correct

Area of a rectangle $= width \times height, Area = 138 \times 83 = 11,454 \ sq.ft$

19) Choice D is correct

$89 \div \frac{1}{8} = 89 \times 8 = 712$

20) Choice C is correct

Let x be the original price of the dress. Then: $22\% \ of \ x = 20.42$
$\frac{22}{100}x = 20.42, x = \frac{100 \times 20.42}{22} \cong \$92.82$

21) Choice D is correct

$\frac{7}{25} = 0.28$

22) Choice B is correct

20% of A is 1,600 Then: $0.2A = 1,600 \rightarrow A = \frac{1,600}{0.2} = 8,000$, 15% of 8,000 is: $0.15 \times 8,000 = 1,200$

23) Choice A is correct

$(5.2 + 9.3 + 1.5) \times x = x$, $16x = x$, Then $x = 0$

24) Choice B is correct

For sum of 6: (1 & 5) and (5 & 1), (2 & 4) and (4 & 2), (3 & 3), therefore we have 5 options. For sum of 9: (3 & 6) and (6 & 3), (4 & 5) and (5 & 4), we have 4 options. To get a sum of 6 or 9 for two dice: $5 + 4 = 9$. Since, we have $6 \times 6 = 36$ total number of options, the probability of getting a sum of 6 and 9 is 9 out of 36 or $\frac{9}{36} = \frac{1}{4}$

25) Choice D is correct

Simplify:

$$\frac{\frac{1}{2} - \frac{x+5}{4}}{\frac{x^2}{2} - \frac{5}{2}} = \frac{\frac{1}{2} - \frac{x+5}{4}}{\frac{x^2 - 5}{2}} = \frac{2(\frac{1}{2} - \frac{x+5}{4})}{x^2 - 5}, \Rightarrow \text{Simplify: } \frac{1}{2} - \frac{x+5}{4} = \frac{-x-3}{4}$$

Then: $\dfrac{2(\frac{-x-3}{4})}{x^2-5} = \dfrac{\frac{-x-3}{2}}{x^2-5} = \dfrac{-x-3}{2(x^2-5)} = \dfrac{-x-3}{2x^2-10}$

26) Choice B is correct

The distance of A to B on the coordinate plane is: $\sqrt{(x_1 - x_2)^2 + (y_1 - y_2)^2} =$ $\sqrt{(10-4)^2 + (11-3)^2} = \sqrt{6^2 + 8^2}, = \sqrt{36 + 64} = \sqrt{100} = 10$
The diameter of the circle is 10 and the radius of the circle is 5. Then: the circumference of the circle is: $2\pi r = 2\pi(5) = 10\pi$

27) Choice D is correct
$2x^2 + 5 = 23$, $2x^2 = 18$, $x^2 = 9$, $x = \pm 3$
28) Choice A is correct

Diameter $= 16$ $inch$, then: Radius $= 8$ $inch$, Area of a circle $= \pi r^2 \Rightarrow A = 3.14(8)^2 = 200.96$ $sq. inch$

29) Choice D is correct

Write a proportion and solve. $\frac{6}{36} = \frac{x}{180} \rightarrow x = \frac{6 \times 180}{36} = 30$

30) Choice B is correct

$56.78 \div 0.06 = 946.33$

31) Choice A is correct

The mean of the data is 10. Then:
$$\frac{x+9+14+12+}{5} = 10 \rightarrow x + 40 = 50 \qquad \rightarrow \qquad x = 50 - 40 = 10$$

32) Choice D is correct

The difference of the file added, and the file deleted is: $652{,}159 - 599{,}986 = 52{,}173$
$937{,}036 + 52{,}173 = 989{,}209$ bytes

33) Choice B is correct

$5 \ days \ 19 \ hours \ 35 \ minutes - 3 \ days \ 12 \ hours \ 22 \ minutes$
$$= 2 \ days \ \ 7 \ hours \ \ 13 \ minutes$$

34) Choice A is correct

Formula of triangle area $= \frac{1}{2}(base \times height)$.Since the angles are $45 - 45 - 90$, then this is an isosceles triangle, meaning that the base and height of the triangle are equal.

A. Triangle area $= \frac{1}{2}(base \times height) = \frac{1}{2}(2 \times 2) = 2 \ square \ feet$

35) Choice C is correct

$50\% \ of \ 84 = 42, 84 + 42 = 126$

36) Choice C is correct

Only choice C represents the statement "twice the difference between 6 times H and 3 gives 30". $2(6H - 3) = 30$

37) Choice D is correct

The area of the circle is $16\pi \ cm^2$, then, its diameter is $8cm$. $area \ of \ a \ circle = \pi r^2 = 16\pi \rightarrow r^2 = 16 \rightarrow r = 4$. Radius of the circle is 4 and diameter is twice of it, 8.
One side of the square equals to the diameter of the circle. Then:
$Area \ of \ square = side \times side = 8 \times 8 = 64 \ cm^2$

38) Choice D is correct

$x^{\frac{1}{2}}$equals to the root of x. Then: $10 + x^{\frac{1}{2}} = 14 \rightarrow 10 + \sqrt{x} = 14 \rightarrow \sqrt{x} = 4 \rightarrow x = 16$
$x = 16$ and $15 \times x$ equals: $15 \times 16 = 240$

39) Choice D is correct.

When a point is reflected over x axes, the (y) coordinate of that point changes to $(-y)$ while its x coordinate remains the same. $C \ (7,9) \rightarrow C' \ (7,-9)$

40) Choice D is correct.

A set of ordered pairs represents y as a function of x if: $x_1 = x_2 \rightarrow y_1 = y_2$
In choice A: $(3, -2)$ and $(3, 7)$ are ordered pairs with same x and different y, therefore y isn't a function of x.
In choice B: $(4, 2)$ and $(4, 7)$ are ordered pairs with same x and different y, therefore y isn't a function of x.
In choice C: $(5, 7)$ and $(5, 18)$ are ordered pairs with same x and different y, therefore y isn't a function of x.

41) Choice D is correct

If the length of the box is $27 \; cm$, then the width of the box is one third of it, $9 \; cm$, and the height of the box is $3 \; cm$ (one third of the width). The volume of the box is:
$V = length \times width \times height = (27)(9)(3) = 729 \; cm^3$

42) Choice B is correct

The area of the square is 36 square inches. $Area \; of \; square = side \times side = 6 \times 6 = 36$
The length of the square is increased by 5 inches and its width decreased by 3 inches. Then, its area equals: $Area \; of \; rectangle = width \times length = 11 \times 3 = 33$
The area of the square will be decreased by 3 square inches. $36 - 33 = 3 \; sq \; decreased$

43) Choice B is correct

Write a proportion and solve. $\frac{2}{3} = \frac{x}{90}$, Use cross multiplication: $3x = 180 \rightarrow x = 60$

44) Choice A is correct

Number of squares equal to: $\frac{54 \times 12}{3 \times 3} = 18 \times 4 = 72$

45) Choice C is correct

David's weekly salary is \$220 plus 8% of \$1,100. Then: $8\% \; of \; 1,100 = 0.08 \times 1,100 = 88$
$220 + 88 = \$308$

46) Choice D is correct

$4x^2y^3 + 5x^3y^5 - (5x^2y^3 - 2x^3y^5) = = 4x^2y^3 + 5x^3y^5 - 5x^2y^3 + 2x^3y^5) = -x^2y^3 + 7\,x^3y^5$

47) Choice C is correct

Let P be circumference of circle A, then; $2\pi r_A = 18\pi \rightarrow r_A = 9, r_A = 3r_B \rightarrow r_B = \frac{9}{3} = 3 \rightarrow$ Area of circle B is; $\qquad \pi r_B^2 = 9\pi$

ISEE Upper Level Practice Test 2
Quantitative Reasoning

1) Choice B is correct

Find the value of each choice:
$2 \times 2 \times 5 \times 7 = 140, 2 \times 2 \times 2 \times 2 \times 5 \times 7 = 560, 2 \times 7 = 14, 2 \times 2 \times 2 \times 5 \times 7 = 280$

2) Choice B is correct

Recall that the formula for the average is: $Average = \frac{sum\ of\ data}{number\ of\ data}$

First, compute the total weight of all balls in the basket: $25 = \frac{total\ weig}{20\ balls}$

$25g \times 20 = total\ weight = 500\ g$

Next, find the total weight of the 5 largest marbles: $40g = \frac{total\ weigh}{5\ marbles}$

$40\ g \times 5 = total\ weight = 200\ g$

The total weight of the heaviest balls is $200\ g$. Then, the total weight of the remaining 15 balls is $300\ g$. $500\ g - 200\ g = 300\ g$.

The average weight of the remaining balls: $Average = \frac{300\ g}{15\ marbles} = 20\ g\ per\ ball$

3) Choice C is correct

$(5x + 8) - (5x - 3) = 5x - 5x + 8 + 3 = 11$

4) Choice D is correct

Write a proportion and solve. $\frac{5i}{100feet} = \frac{18in}{x} \rightarrow x = \frac{100 \times 18}{5} = 360$ feet

5) Choice D is correct

Let x be all expenses, then $\frac{22}{100}x = \$660 \rightarrow x = \frac{100 \times \$660}{22} = \$3,000$

He spent for his rent: $\frac{27}{100} \times \$3,000 = \$810$

6) Choice D is correct

There is not enough information to determine the answer of the question. An average speed represents a distance divided by time and it does not provide information about the speed at specific time. Alice could drove exactly 55 miles per hour from start to finish, or she could drive 65 miles per hour for half of distance and 45 miles per hour for the other half.

7) Choice A is correct

Area of the circle is less than $64\ \pi$. Use the formula of areas of circles.
$Area = \pi r^2 \Rightarrow 64\ \pi > \pi r^2 \Rightarrow 64 > r^2 \Rightarrow r < 8$

Radius of the circle is less than 8. Let's put 8 for the radius. Now, use the circumference formula: $Circumference = 2\pi r = 2\pi (8) = 16\pi$. Since the radius of the circle is less than 8. Then, the circumference of the circle must be less than 16π. Only choice A is less than 16π.

8) Choice C is correct

The percentage discount is the reduction in price divided by the original price. The difference between original price and sale price is: $\$12.65 - \$7.35 = \$5.3$

The percentage discount is this difference divided by the original price: $\$5.3 \div \$12.65 \cong 0.42$

Convert the decimal to a percentage by multiplying by 100%: $0.42 \times 100\% = 42\%$

9) Choice C is correct

The smallest possible value of $f(x)$ will occur when $x = 0$. Since x^2 is always positive, any positive or negative value of x will make the value of $f(x)$ greater than 5. Substitute 0 for x and evaluate the expression: $f(0) = (0)^2 + 5 = 5$

10) Choice D is correct

There are 2 sets of values, one set from 1 to n, and the other set from $n + 1$ to $2n$. Since the second set begins immediately after the first set, the two sets can be combined. The sum of the positive integers from 1 to $2n$ inclusive is equal to the sum of the positive integers from 1 to n plus the sum of the positive integers from $n + 1$ to $2n$: $2,250 + 4,356 = 6,606$

11) Choice C is correct

Let's review the choices provided:

A. Number of books sold in April is: 380

Number of books sold in July is: $760 \rightarrow \frac{380}{760} = \frac{38}{76} = \frac{1}{2}$

B. number of books sold in July is: 760

Half the number of books sold in May is: $\frac{1140}{2} = 570 \rightarrow 760 > 570$

C. number of books sold in June is: 190

Half the number of books sold in April is: $\frac{380}{2} = 190 \rightarrow 190 = 190$

D. $380 + 190 = 570 < 760$

Only choice C is correct.

12) Choice C is correct

The median of a set of data is the value located in the middle of the data set. Combine the 2 sets provided, and organize them in ascending order: $\{1, 3, 4, 6, 8, 10, 12, 14, 15, 17\}$

Since there are an even number of items in the resulting list, the median is the average of the two middle numbers. $Median = (8 + 10) \div 2 = 9$

13) Choice D is correct

Let x be the number of current stamps in the collection. Then: $\frac{6}{5}x - x = 100 \rightarrow \frac{1}{5}x = 100 \rightarrow$ $x = 500$, 50% more of 500 is: $500 + 0.50 \times 500 = 500 + 250 = 750$

14) Choice D is correct

If 17 balls are removed from the bag at random, there will be one ball in the bag. The probability of choosing a brown ball is 1 out of 18. Therefore, the probability of not choosing a brown ball is 17 out of 18 and the probability of having not a brown ball after removing 17 balls is the same.

15) Choice B is correct

$(x^2 - y^2) = (x - y)(x + y)$, Then: $x^2 - y^2 = 5 \times 8 = 40$

16) Choice C is correct

The ratio of boy to girls is $4 : 7$. Therefore, there are 4 boys out of 11 students. To find the answer, first divide the total number of students by 11, then multiply the result by 4.
$44 \div 11 = 4 \Rightarrow 4 \times 4 = 16$, There are 16 boys and $28 \, (44 - 16)$ girls. So, $12 \, (28 - 16)$ more boys should be enrolled to make the ratio $1 : 1$.

17) Choice B is correct

The formula for the area of a rectangle is: $Area = Width \times Length$
It is given that $L = 4 \, W$ and that $A = 196$ square inches. Substitute the given values into our equation and solve for W: $196 = w \times 4w$, $196 = 4w^2$, $w^2 = 49$,$w = 7$. It is given that $L = 4W$, therefore, $L = 4 \times 7 = 28$, The perimeter of a rectangle is: $2L + 2W$
Perimeter $= 2 \times 28 + 2 \times 7$,   Perimeter $= 70$ inches

18) Choice B is correct

The sum of 8 numbers is greater than 160 and less than 240. Then, the average of the 8 numbers must be greater than 20 and less than 30. $\frac{160}{8} < x < \frac{240}{8}$
$20 < x < 30$, The only choice that is between 20 and 30 is 25.

19) Choice B is correct
In order to solve for the variable b, first take square roots on both sides: $\sqrt{a} = \frac{cz}{b}$, then multiply both sides by b: $b\sqrt{a} = cz$, Now, divide both sides by $\sqrt{a}$: $b = \frac{cz}{\sqrt{a}}$

20) Choice B is correct
If two triangles are similar, then the ratios of corresponding sides are equal.
$\frac{AC}{AE} = \frac{BC}{DE} = \frac{18}{9} = 2, \frac{AC}{AE} = 2$
This ratio can be used to find the length of AC: $AC = 2 \times AE$,$AC = 2 \times 9$,$AC = 18$
The length of AE is given as 9 and we now know the length of AC is 18, therefore:
$EC = AC - AE$,$EC = 18 - 9$, $EC = 9$

21) Choice B is correct
Let x be number of gallons the tank can hold when it is full. Then: $\frac{2}{5}x = 25 \rightarrow x = \frac{5}{2} \times 25 = 62.5$

22) Choice A is correct
The average is the sum of all terms divided by the number of terms.

$15 + 25 + 27 = 67$, $67 \div 3 = 22.33$. This is greater than 20.

23) Choice B is correct

Since both columns have 675 as a factor, we can ignore that number.
$11 \times 24 = 264$, $18 \times 17 = 306$. Column B is greater

24) Choice D is correct

Since x is an integer and can be positive and negative, then the relationship cannot be determined from the information given. Let's choose some values for x.

$x = 1$, then the value in column A is greater. $1 > \frac{1}{-2}$

Let's choose a negative value for x. $x = -1$, then the value in column B is greater.

$-1 < \frac{-1}{-2} \rightarrow -1 < \frac{1}{2}$

25) Choice A is correct

First, find the values of x in both columns.

Column A: $6|2x - 4| = 6 \rightarrow |2x - 4| = 1$

$2x - 4$ can be 1 or -1.

$2x - 4 = 1 \rightarrow 2x = 5 \rightarrow x = \frac{5}{2}$

$2x - 4 = -1 \rightarrow 2x = 3 \rightarrow x = \frac{3}{2}$

Column B: $6|2x + 4| = 6 \rightarrow |2x + 4| = 1$

$2x + 4$ can be 1 or -1.

$2x + 4 = 1 \rightarrow 2x = -3 \rightarrow x = -\frac{3}{2}$

$2x + 4 = -1 \rightarrow 2x = -5 \rightarrow x = -\frac{5}{2}$

The greatest value of x in column A is $\frac{5}{2}$ and the greatest value of x in column B is $-\frac{3}{2}$.

26) Choice D is correct

Simplify both columns.

Column A: $(x)^3(x)^4 = x^7$

Column B: $(x^3)^4 = x^{12}$

Column A evaluates to x^7 and Column B evaluates to x^{12}. In the case where $x = 0$, the two columns will be equal, but if $x = 2$, the two columns will not be equal. Consequently, the relationship cannot be determined.

27) Choice D is correct

The probability that an event will occur + the probability that that event will NOT occur must equal 1. Since we don't have any numerical information about the probability, it is possible that the probability that event x occurs is 25%, 50% or any other percent. The probability that event x will not occur will always be 100% minus the probability that event x does occur. Because both columns can exhibit a range of values, the relationship cannot be determined.

28) Choice C is correct

Column A: $2^2 = 4$, Column B: $\sqrt[3]{64} = 4$ (recall that $4^3 = 16$)

29) Choice A is correct

A number raised to the exponent $\frac{1}{2}$ is the same thing as evaluating the square root of the number. Therefore: $(59)^{\frac{1}{2}} = \sqrt{59}$, Since $\sqrt{64}$ is greater than $\sqrt{59}$, column A ($\sqrt{64} = 8$) is greater than $\sqrt{59}$.

30) Choice A is correct

Let x be the original price of the sport jacket. The selling price of a sport jacket including 25% discount is \$51. Then: $x - 0.25x = 51 \rightarrow 0.75x = 51 \rightarrow x = \frac{51}{0.75} = 68$
The original price of the jacket is \$68 which is greater than column B (\$67).

31) Choice B is correct

The value of x has to be less than 50, which is less than 60. Column B is greater.
Recall that when the positive powers of numbers between 0 and 1 increases, the value of the number decrease. For example: $(0.5)^2 > (0.5)^3 \rightarrow 0.25 > 0.125$. So, $(0.69)^{33} > (0.69)^{34}$

32) Choice B is correct

Because of the word "and" the events described in each column must be calculated separately and then multiplied: For column A: Probability of rolling a 6: $\frac{1}{6}$
Probability of getting heads: $\frac{1}{2}, \frac{1}{6} \times \frac{1}{2} = \frac{1}{12}$.
For column B: Probability of an even number: $\frac{3}{6} = \frac{1}{2}$
Probability of getting a spade: $\frac{13}{52} = \frac{1}{4}, \frac{1}{2} \times \frac{1}{4} = \frac{1}{8}$
Since $\frac{1}{8}$ is a larger number than $\frac{1}{12}$, Colum B is greater

33) Choice C is correct

To raise a quantity to a negative power, invert the numerator and denominator, and then raise the base to the indicated power. Therefore: $(\frac{5}{1})^{-2} = (\frac{1}{5})^2$, The Columns are the same value.

34) Choice A is correct

First, simplify the inequality: $x + 2 > 5x \rightarrow 2 > 4x \rightarrow \frac{2}{4} > x \rightarrow \frac{1}{2} > x$
Since x is less than $\frac{1}{2}$, and x can be 0 (greater than -1) or -2 (less than -1), the relationship cannot be determined.

35) Choice A is correct

Sum of one quarter, two nickels, and three pennies is: $\$0.25 + 2(\$0.05) + \$0.03 = \$0.38$

36) Choice A is correct

Let's consider the properties of odd and even integers:

$Odd +/- Odd = Even$

$Even +/- Even = Even$

$Odd +/- Even = Odd$

$Odd \times Odd = Odd$

$Even \times Even = Even$

$Odd \times Even = Even$

Now let's review the columns. For column A: $(x + y)^2 - y$

$(odd + even)^2 - even$

$(odd)^2 - even$

$(odd)(odd) - even$

$odd - even$

odd

For Column B:

$(y)(x - y)$

$(even)(odd - even)$

$(even)(odd)$

$even$

Since an odd number is considered greater according to the problem statement, the answer is A.

37) Choice D is correct

Factor the expression if possible. Begin by moving all terms to one side before factoring:

$x^2 - 5x - 8 = 6$

$x^2 - 5x - 14 = 0$

To factor this quadratic, find two numbers that multiply to -14 and sum to -5:

$(x - 7)(x + 2) = 0$

Set each expression in parentheses equal to 0 and solve: $x - 7 = 0$,$x = 7$

$x + 2 = 0$,$x = -2$

Quadratic equations can have TWO possible solutions. Since one of these is greater than 0 and one of them is less than 0, we cannot determine the relationship between the columns.

ISEE Upper Level Practice Test 2
Mathematics Achievement

1)   Choice B is correct

Subtract $\dfrac{1}{6b}$ and $\dfrac{1}{b^2}$ from both sides of the equation. Then:

$$\frac{1}{6b^2} + \frac{1}{6b} = \frac{1}{b^2} \rightarrow \frac{1}{6b^2} - \frac{1}{b^2} = -\frac{1}{6b}$$

Multiply both numerator and denominator of the fraction $\dfrac{1}{b^2}$ by 6. Then:

$$\frac{1}{6b^2} - \frac{6}{6b^2} = -\frac{1}{6b}$$

Simplify the first side of the equation: $-\dfrac{5}{6b^2} = -\dfrac{1}{6b}$

Use cross multiplication method: $30b = 6b^2 \rightarrow 30 = 6b \rightarrow b = 5$

2) Choice B is correct

First, multiply both sides of inequality by 7. Then: $\dfrac{|3+x|}{7} \leq 5 \rightarrow |3+x| \leq 35$

$-35 \leq 3 + x \leq 35 \rightarrow -35 - 3 \leq x \leq 35 - 3 \rightarrow -38 \leq x \leq 32$

3) Choice B is correct

Plug in the value of $x = 30$ into both equations. Then: $C(x) = x^2 + 2x = (30)^2 + 2(30) = 900 + 60 = 960, R(x) = 40x = 40 \times 30 = 1,200 , 1,200 - 960 = 240.$ So, the profit is $240.

4) Choice D is correct

From choices provided, only choice D is correct. $E = 4 + A, A = S - 3$

5) Choice D is correct

Let x be the integer. Then: $2x - 5 = 83$, Add 5 both sides: $2x = 88$, Divide both sides by 2: $x = 44$

6) Choice A is correct.

Plug in each pair of numbers in the equation. The answer should be 14.

A. $(2, 1)$: $4(2) + 6(1) = 14$ Yes!
B. $(-1, 2)$: $4(-1) + 6(2) = 8$ No!
C. $(-2, 2)$: $4(-2) + 6(2) = 4$ No!
D. $(2, 2)$: $4(2) + 6(2) = 20$ No!

7) Choice B is correct

The sum of supplement angles is $180°$. Let x be that angle. Therefore, $x + 5x = 180°$
$6x = 180°$, divide both sides by 6: $x = 30°$

8) Choice B is correct

$x\% \ 24 = 1.2, \dfrac{x}{100} 24 = 1.2 \rightarrow x = \dfrac{1.2 \times 100}{24} = 5$

9) Choice D is correct

Use Pythagorean Theorem: $a^2 + b^2 = c^2$, $6^2 + 8^2 = c^2 \Rightarrow 100 = c^2 \Rightarrow c = 10 \ cm$

10) Choice D is correct

Simplify. $6x^2y^3(2x^2y)^3 = 6x^2y^3(8x^6y^3) = 48x^8y^6$

11) Choice C is correct

$23\ hours\ =\ 82,800\ seconds, 1520\ minutes\ =\ 91,200\ seconds, 2\ days\ =\ 48\ hours\ =\ 172,800\ seconds$

12) Choice C is correct

Let's review the choices provided:
A. $(5 \times 10^3) + (2 \times 10^2) + (3 \times 10) = 5,000 + 200 + 30 = 5,230$
B. $(5 \times 10^2) + (2 \times 10^1) - 5 = 500 + 20 - 5 = 515$
C. $(5 \times 10^2) + (2 \times 10^1) + 3 = 500 + 20 + 3 = 523$
D. $(5 \times 10^1) + (2 \times 10^2) + 3 = 50 + 200 + 3 = 253$
Only choice C equals to 523.

13) Choice C is correct

$$\frac{4}{400} = \frac{x}{960}, x = \frac{4 \times 960}{400} = \$\ 9.6$$

14) Choice C is correct

Area of a circle equals: $A = \pi r^2$
The new diameter is 30% larger than the original then the new radius is also 30% larger than the original. 30% larger than r is $1.3r$. Then, the area of larger circle is:
$A = \pi r^2 = \pi(1.3r)^2 = \pi(1.69r^2) = 1.69\pi r^2$. $1.69\pi r^2$ is 69% bigger than πr^2.

15) Choice B is correct

$C = 2\pi r.\ C = 2\pi \times 4 = 8\pi, \pi = 3.14 \rightarrow C = 8\pi = 25.12$ inches

16) Choice A is correct

First draw an isosceles triangle. Remember that two sides of the triangle are equal.
Let put a for the legs. Then: Use Pythagorean theorem to find the value of a:
$a^2 + b^2 = c^2 \rightarrow a^2 + a^2 = 6^2$
Simplify: $2a^2 = 36 \rightarrow a^2 = 18 \rightarrow a = \sqrt{18}$
$a = \sqrt{18} \Rightarrow$ area of the triangle is $= \frac{1}{2}(\sqrt{18} \times \sqrt{18}) = \frac{1}{2} \times 18 = 9\ cm^2$

Isosceles right triangl

17) Choice B is correct

The area of the non-shaded region is equal to the area of the bigger rectangle subtracted by the area of smaller rectangle. Area of the bigger rectangle $= 12 \times 16 = 192$
Area of the smaller rectangle $= 10 \times 4 = 40$, Area of the non-shaded region $= 192 - 40 = 152$

18) Choice B is correct

$79.22 \div 0.05 = 1,584.4$

19) Choice B is correct

$$3\frac{1}{3} - 2\frac{5}{6} = 3\frac{2}{6} - 2\frac{5}{6} = \frac{20}{6} - \frac{17}{6} = \frac{3}{6} = \frac{1}{2}$$

20) Choice C is correct

Let's review the choices provided. Put the values of x and y in the equation.
A. $(1, 2)$ $\Rightarrow x = 1 \Rightarrow y = 2$ This is true!
B. $(-2, -13)$ $\Rightarrow x = -2 \Rightarrow y = -13$ This is true!
C. $(3, 18)$ $\Rightarrow x = 3 \Rightarrow y = 12$ This is not true!
D. $(2, 7)$ $\Rightarrow x = 2 \Rightarrow y = 7$ This is true!

21) Choice C is correct

To find total number of miles driven by Ed that week, you only need to subtract 40,907 from 41,053. $41,053 - 40,907 = 146\ miles$

22) Choice D is correct

To find the maximum value of y, the expression $(x - 2)^2$ must be equal to 0. Because it has a negative sign. Since $x - 2$ is to the power of 2, it cannot be negative. To get 0 for the expression $(x - 2)^2$, x must be 2. Plug in 2 for x in the equation: $y = -(x - 2)^2 + 6 \rightarrow y = -(2 - 2)^2 + 6 = 6$. The maximum value of y is 6.

23) Choice B is correct

$\begin{cases} -2x - y = -9 \\ 5x - 2y = 18 \end{cases} \Rightarrow$ Multiplication (-2) in first equation $\Rightarrow \begin{cases} 4x + 2y = 18 \\ 5x - 2y = 18 \end{cases}$
Add two equations together $\Rightarrow 9x = 36 \Rightarrow x = 4$ then: $y = 1$

24) Choice A is correct

First draw an isosceles triangle. Remember that two sides of the triangle are equal.
Let put a for the legs. Then: Isosceles right triangle
$a = 6 \Rightarrow$ area of the triangle is $= \frac{1}{2}(6 \times 6) = \frac{36}{2} = 18\ cm^2$

25) Choice A is correct

Factor each trinomial $x^2 - 2x - 8$ and $x^2 - 6x + 8$
$x^2 - 2x - 8 \Rightarrow (x - 4)(x + 2)$, $x^2 - 6x + 8 \Rightarrow (x - 2)(x - 4)$
The common factor of both expressions is $(x - 4)$.

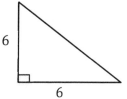

6

6

26) Choice B is correct

$\frac{13}{25} = 0.52$

27) Choice C is correct

$x + y = 12$, Then: $8x + 8y = 8(x + y) = 8 \times 12 = 96$

28) Choice B is correct

$$\begin{array}{r} 37 \text{ hr. } 25 \text{ min.} \\ -\ \underline{24 \text{ hr. } 38 \text{ min.}} \\ 12 \text{ hr. } 47 \text{ min} \end{array}$$

29) Choice C is correct

$\frac{450}{15} = 30 \ miles \ per \ gallon$

30) Choice C is correct

First, convert all measurement to foot. One foot is 12 inches. Then: 8 inches $= \frac{8}{12} = \frac{2}{3}$ feet

The volume flower box is: $length \times width \times height = 2 \times \frac{2}{3} \times 2 = \frac{8}{3}$ cubic feet.

31) Choice D is correct

$\frac{x^3}{16} \quad \Rightarrow$ reciprocal is : $\frac{16}{x^3}$

32) Choice C is correct

Use interest rate formula: $Interest = principal \times rate \times time = 1,200 \times 0.05 \times 1 = \$60$

33) Choice D is correct

Ellis travels $\frac{3}{5}$ of 80 hours. $\frac{3}{5} \times 80 = 48$, Ellis will be on the road for 48 hours.

34) Choice A is correct

Plug in the values of x and y in the expression:
$2x^2(y + 4) = 2(0.6)^2(6 + 4) = 2 \ (0.36)(10) = 7.2$

35) Choice B is correct

Let's write equations based on the information provided:
$Michelle = Karen - 9$
$Michelle = David - 4$
$Karen + Michelle + David = 82$
$Karen - 9 = Michelle \Rightarrow Karen = Michelle + 9$
$Karen + Michelle + David = 82$
Now, replace the ages of Karen and David by Michelle. Then:
$Michelle + 9 + Michelle + Michelle + 4 = 82$
$3Michelle + 13 = 82 \Rightarrow 3Michelle = 82 - 13$
$3Michelle = 69$
$Michelle = 23$

36) Choice C is correct

$A = bh, \qquad A = 2 \times 2.4 = 4.8 \ square \ feet$

37) Choice D is correct

To find the discount, multiply the number by $(100\% - rate\ of\ discount)$.
Therefore, for the first discount we get: $(200)\,(100\% - 25\%) = (200)\,(0.75)$
For the next 15% discount: $(200)\,(0.75)\,(0.85)$

38) Choice D is correct

The ratio of boys to girls is $3:7$. Therefore, there are 3 boys out of 10 students. To find the answer, first divide the number of boys by 3, then multiply the result by 10.
$180 \div 3 = 60 \Rightarrow 60 \times 10 = 600$

39) Choice A is correct

Write a proportion and solve for the missing number. $\frac{32}{12} = \frac{6}{x} \rightarrow 32x = 6 \times 12 = 72$

$32x = 72 \rightarrow x = \dfrac{72}{32} = 2.25\ ft$

40) Choice B is correct.

To find the area of the shaded region subtract smaller circle from bigger circle.
$S_{\text{bigger}} - S_{\text{smaller}} = \pi\big(r_{\text{bigger}}\big)^2 - \pi\,(r_{\text{smaller}})^2 \Rightarrow S_{\text{bigger}} - S_{\text{smaller}} = \pi(6)^2 - \pi\,(4)^2 \Rightarrow$
$36\,\pi - 16\pi = 20\,\pi\ inch^2$

41) Choice C is correct.
To add two matrices, first we need to find corresponding members from each matrix.
$\begin{vmatrix} 3 & 6 \\ -1 & -3 \\ -5 & -1 \end{vmatrix} + \begin{vmatrix} 0 & -1 \\ 6 & 0 \\ 2 & 3 \end{vmatrix} = \begin{vmatrix} 3 & 5 \\ 5 & -3 \\ -3 & 2 \end{vmatrix}$

42) Choice C is correct
The area of a $18\ feet\ x\ 18\ feet$ room is 324 square feet. $18 \times 18 = 324$
43) Choice C is correct

Use FOIL (First, Out, In, Last). $(3x + 3)(x + 5) = 3x^2 + 15x + 3x + 15 = 3x^2 + 18x + 15$

44) Choice B is correct

Plug in the values of x and y in the equation: $5\,\blacksquare\,11 = \sqrt{5^2 + 11} = \sqrt{25 + 11} = \sqrt{36} = 6$

45) Choice A is correct

Let x be the capacity of one tank. Then, $\frac{2}{5}x = 200 \rightarrow x = \frac{200 \times 5}{2} = 500$ Liters
The amount of water in three tanks is equal to: $3 \times 500 = 1,500$ Liters

46) Choice B is correct

$Average = \frac{sum\ of\ terms}{number\ of\ terms}$, The sum of the weight of all girls is: $18 \times 60 = 1,080\ kg$, The sum of the weight of all boys is: $32 \times 62 = 1,984\ kg$. The sum of the weight of all students is: $1,080 + 1,984 = 3,064\ kg$, $Average = \frac{3064}{50} = 61.28\ kg$

47) Choice B is correct

$\frac{45}{100} \times 820 = x$, $x = 369$, $x = 369$.

ISEE Upper Level Math Practice Test 3

Quantitative Reasoning

1) Choice D is correct

$2y + 6 < 30 \rightarrow 2y < 30 - 6 \rightarrow 2y < 24 \rightarrow y < 12$, Only choice D (8) is less than 12.

2) Choice C is correct

A factor must divide evenly into its multiple. 16 cannot be a factor of 90 because 90 divided by $16 = 5.625$

3) Choice B is correct

The diagonal of the square is 6 meters. Let x be the side.
Use Pythagorean Theorem: $a^2 + b^2 = c^2$
$x^2 + x^2 = 6^2 \Rightarrow 2x^2 = 6^2 \Rightarrow 2x^2 = 36 \Rightarrow x^2 = 18 \Rightarrow x = \sqrt{18}$
The area of the square is: $\sqrt{18} \times \sqrt{18} = 18\ m^2$

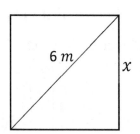

4) Choice B is correct

To find what percent A is of B, divide A by B, then multiply that number by 100%:
$13.26 \div 58.56 = 0.2264 \times 100\% = 22.64\%$,   This is approximately 22%.

5) Choice C is correct

$Probability = \frac{number\ of\ desired\ outcomes}{number\ of\ total\ outcomes}$
In this case, a desired outcome is selecting either a red or a yellow marble. Combine the number of red and yellow marbles: $9 + 6 = 15$, and divide this by the total number of marbles: $7 + 9 + 6 = 22$. The probability is $\frac{15}{22}$.

6) Choice B is correct

Begin by calculating James's total earnings after 20 hours: $20\ hours \times \$8.500\ per\ hour = \$170$, Next, divide this total by Jacob's hourly rate to find the number of hours Jacob would need to work: $\$170 \div \$10.00\ per\ hour = 17\ hours$

7) Choice C is correct

The total cost of the phone call can be represented by the equation: $TC = \$5.00 + \$0.5x$, where x is the duration of the call after the first five minutes. In this case, $x = 30$. Substitute the known values into the equation and solve: $TC = \$5.00 + \$0.5 \times 30$
$TC = \$5.00 + \$15.00$, $TC = \$20.00$

8) Choice B is correct

Let b be the amount of time Alec can do the job, then,
$$\frac{1}{a} + \frac{1}{b} = \frac{1}{50} \rightarrow \frac{1}{150} + \frac{1}{b} = \frac{1}{50} \rightarrow \frac{1}{b} = \frac{1}{50} - \frac{1}{150} = \frac{2}{150} = \frac{1}{75}$$
Then: $b = 75$ minutes

9) Choice A is correct

First, find the number. Let x be the number. Write the equation and solve for x. 150% of a number is 75, then: $1.5 \times x = 75 \rightarrow x = 75 \div 1.5 = 50$, 90% of 50 is: $0.9 \times 50 = 45$

10) Choice B is correct

The length of MN is equal to: $4x + 6x = 10x$, Then: $10x = 50 \rightarrow x = \frac{50}{10} = 5$
The length of ON is equal to: $6x = 6 \times 5 = 30\ cm$

11) Choice A is correct
The distance on the map is proportional to the actual distance between the two cities. Use the information to set up a proportion and then solve for the unknown number of actual miles:
$\frac{14\,miles}{\frac{1}{2}\,inches} = \frac{x\,miles}{18\,inches}$,   Cross multiply and simplify to solve for the x:

$\frac{14 \times 18}{\frac{1}{2}} = x\,miles \rightarrow \frac{252}{\frac{1}{2}} = 252 \times 2 = 504\,miles$

12) Choice C is correct
Number of Mathematics books: $0.35 \times 700 = 245$
Number of English books: $0.13 \times 700 = 91$
Product of number of Mathematics and number of English books: $245 \times 91 = 22,295$

13) Choice D is correct

If each book weighs $\frac{1}{6}$ pound, then $1\ pound = 6\ books$. To find the number of books in 60 pounds, simply multiply this 6 by 60: $60 \times 6 = 360$

14) Choice B is correct

Write equations based on the information provided in the question:
$Emily = Daniel, Emily = 6\ Claire, Daniel = 15 + Claire$
$Emily = Daniel \rightarrow Emily = 15 + Claire$
$Emily = 6\ Claire \rightarrow 6\ Claire = 15 + Claire \rightarrow 6\ Claire - Claire = 15$
$5\ Claire = 15, Claire = 3$

15) Choice A is correct

Begin by examining the sequence to find the pattern. The difference between 3 and 6 is 3; moving from 6 to 11 requires 5 to be added; moving from 11 to 18 requires 7 to be added. The pattern emerges here — adding by consecutive odd integers. The 5th term is equal to $18 + 9 = 27$, and the 6th term is equal to $27 + 11 = 38$.

16) Choice A is correct

The general slope-intercept form of the equation of a line is $y = mx + b$, where m is the slope and b is the y-intercept. By substitution of the given point and given slope: $-3 = (3)(2) + b$, So, $b = -3 - 6 = -9$, and the required equation is $y = 3x - 9$.

17) Choice D is correct

Multiplying each side of $-4x - y = 8$ by 2 gives $-8x - 2y = 16$. Adding each side of $-8x - 2y = 16$ to the corresponding side of $8x + 6y = 20$ gives $4y = 36$ or $y = 9$. Finally, substituting 9 for y in $8x + 6y = 20$ gives $8x + 6(9) = 20$ or $x = -\frac{17}{4}$.

18) Choice B is correct

The question is this: 530.20 is what percent of 631? Use percent formula:
$Part = \frac{percent}{100} \times whole,$
$530.20 = \frac{percent}{100} \times 631 \to 530.20 = \frac{percent \times 631}{100} \to 53020 = percent \times 631$
Then, Percent $= \frac{53020}{631} = 84.02$
530.20 is 84% of 631. Therefore, the discount is: $100\% - 84\% = 16\%$

19) Choice A is correct

Let x be the number. Write the equation and solve for x. $\frac{3}{2} \times 20 = \frac{5}{2}x \to \frac{3 \times 20}{2} = \frac{5x}{2}$, use cross multiplication to solve for x. $2 \times 60 = 5x \times 2 \Rightarrow 120 = 10x \Rightarrow x = 12$

20) Choice A is correct

Let's choose $100 for the sales of the supermarket. If the sales increases by 11 percent in April, the final amount of sales at the end of April will be $100 + (11\%) \times (\$100) = \$111$.
If sales then decreased by 11 percent in May, the final amount of sales at the end of August will be $111 - (\$111) \times (11\%) = \$98.79$
The final sales of $98 is 98% of the original price of $100. Therefore, the sales decreased by 2% overall.

21) Choice B is correct

The time it takes to drive from city A to city B is: $\frac{2700}{74} = 36.48$

22) Choice D is correct

First find the value of x in the equation: $x^2 = 8 \rightarrow x = \sqrt{8}$, or $x = -\sqrt{8}$. Since $\sqrt{8}$ is bigger than 2 and $-\sqrt{8}$ is smaller than 2. Then: the relationship cannot be determined from the information given.

23) Choice C is correct

Find the value of the functions in each column.
Column A: $4\diamondsuit5 = 4^2 - 2(4)(5) + 5^2 = 16 - 40 + 25 = 1$,
Column B: $5\diamondsuit4 = 5^2 - 2(5)(4) + 4^2 = 25 - 40 + 16 = 1$

The two quantities are equal

24) Choice B is correct

Column A: $\frac{16+22+24+36+}{5} = \frac{138}{5} = 27.6$, Column B: $\frac{28+33+38+4}{4} = \frac{141}{4} = 35.25$

25) Choice D is correct

Let's plug in a value for x and compare the values in both columns.
$$x = -1$$
Column A: $\frac{1}{x+1} = \frac{1}{-1+1} = \frac{1}{0}$, this is undefined.

Column B: $\frac{2}{x+2} = \frac{2}{-1+2} = \frac{2}{1} = 2$
The relationship cannot be determined from the information given

26) Choice D is correct

First, solve the expression for x. $\frac{x}{3} = y^2 \rightarrow x = 3y^2$
Plug in different values for y and find the values of x.
Let's choose $y = 0 \rightarrow x = 3y^2 \rightarrow x = 3(0)^2 = 0$
The values in Column A and B are equal.
Now, let's choose $y = 1 \rightarrow x = 3y^2 \rightarrow x = 3(1)^2 = 3$
Column A is greater. So, the relationship cannot be determined from the information given.

27) Choice B is correct

Column A: $2x^3 - 3x - 2 = 2(1)^3 - 3(1) - 2 = 2 - 3 - 2 = -3$
Column B: $3x^2 - 2x - 3 = 3(1)^2 - 2(1) - 3 = 3 - 2 - 3 = -2$

28) Choice A is correct

Column A: $8 + 14(7 - 3) = 64$, Column B: $14 + 8(7 - 3) = 46$

29) Choice A is correct

First find the value of x. $\frac{x}{36} = \frac{3}{4} \rightarrow 4x = 3 \times 36 = 108 \rightarrow x = \frac{108}{4} = 27$

Column A: $\dfrac{9}{x} = \dfrac{9}{27} = \dfrac{1}{3}$

30) Choice C is correct

First convert hours to minutes. 3 hours 10 minutes $= 3 \times 60 + 10 = 190$ minutes.
Machine D makes b rolls of steel in 38 minutes. So, it makes 5 sets of b in 190 minutes.
$190 \div 38 = 5$ sets of b.
Machine E operates for 5 hours, making b rolls per hour. So, it makes a total of $5b$ rolls.
The two quantities are equal

31) Choice D is correct

$-1 < y < 4$, Let's choose some values for y. $y = 1$
Column A: $\dfrac{y}{2} = \dfrac{1}{2}$, Column B: $\dfrac{2}{y} = \dfrac{2}{1} = 2$, In this case, column B is bigger.
$y = 3$, Column A: $\dfrac{y}{2} = \dfrac{3}{2}$, Column B: $\dfrac{2}{y} = \dfrac{2}{3}$
In this case, Column A is bigger. So, the relationship cannot be determined from the information given.

32) Choice D is correct

$\dfrac{a}{b} = \dfrac{c}{d}$, here there are two equal fractions. Let's choose some values for these variables. $\dfrac{1}{2} = \dfrac{2}{4}$
In this case, Column A is 3 $(1 + 2)$ and Column B is 6 $(2 + 4)$. Since, we can change the positions of these variables (for example put 2 for a and 4 for b), the relationship cannot be determined from the information given.

33) Choice A is correct

The ratio of boys to girls in a class is 5 to 7. Therefore, ratio of boys to the entire class is 5 out of 12. $\dfrac{5}{12} > \dfrac{1}{3}$

34) Choice B is correct

There are 9 marbles in the jar. Let's calculate each probability individually:
The probability that the first marble is blue $= \dfrac{4}{9}$
The probability that the second marble is blue $= \dfrac{3}{8}$
Column A: The probability that both marbles are blue $= \dfrac{4}{9} \times \dfrac{3}{8} = \dfrac{12}{72} = \dfrac{1}{6}$
The probability that the first marble is green $= \dfrac{5}{9}$
The probability that the second marble is blue $= \dfrac{4}{8} = \dfrac{1}{2}$
Column B: The probability that the first marbles is green, but the second is blue $= \dfrac{5}{9} \times \dfrac{1}{2} = \dfrac{5}{18}$
Column B is greater. $\dfrac{5}{18} > \dfrac{1}{6}$.

35) Choice A is correct

First, let's find the number of digits when the printer prints 100 pages.
If there are 2 digits in each page and the printer prints 100 pages, then, there will be 200 digits.
$100 \times 2 = 200$
However, we know that pages $1 - 9$ have only one digit each, so we must subtract 9 from this total: $200 - 9 = 191$. We also know that the number 100th has three digits not two. So, we must add 1 digit to this total: $191 + 1 = 192$.
It is given that 195 digits were printed, and we know that 100 pages results in 192 digits total, so there must be 101 total pages in the magazine. Column A is greater.

36) Choice B is correct

Column A: The largest number that can be written by rearranging the digits in $381 = 831$
Column B: The largest number that can be written by rearranging the digits in $279 = 972$

37) Choice A is correct

The computer priced $147 includes 5% profit. Let x be the original cost of the computer.
Then: $x + 5\% \; of \; x = 147 \rightarrow x + 0.05x = 147 \rightarrow 1.05x = 147 \rightarrow x = \frac{147}{1.05} = \$140$
Column A is bigger.

ISEE Upper Level Math Practice Test 3

Mathematics Achievement

1) Choice A is correct.

$0.00003379 = \frac{3.379}{100,000} \Rightarrow 3.379 \times 10^{-5}$

2) Choice A is correct

$|10 - (12 \div |1 - 5|)| = |10 - (12 \div |-4|)| = |10 - (12 \div 4)| = |10 - 3| = |7| = 7$

3) Choice A is correct

Use FOIL (First, Out, In, Last) method.
$(x + 4)(x + 5) = x^2 + 5x + 4x + 20 = x^2 + 9x + 20$

4) Choice B is correct

Use quadratic formula: $ax^2 + bx + c = 0$
$x_{1,2} = \frac{-b \pm \sqrt{b^2 - 4ac}}{2a}$
$6x^2 + 16x + 8 \quad \Rightarrow \quad$ then: $a = 6, b = 16$ and $c = 8$

$$x = \frac{-16 + \sqrt{16^2 - 4 \times 6 \times 8}}{2 \times 6} = -\frac{2}{3}$$

$$x = \frac{-16 - \sqrt{16^2 - 4 \times 6 \times 8}}{2 \times 6} = -2$$

5) Choice D is correct

Solve for x. $-2 \leq 2x - 4 < 8 \Rightarrow$ (add 4 all sides) $-2 + 4 \leq 2x - 4 + 4 < 8 + 4 \Rightarrow 2 \leq 2x < 12 \Rightarrow$ (divide all sides by 2) $1 \leq x < 6$. x is between 1 and 6. Choice D represent this inequality.

6)   Choice C is correct

Simplify: $1 - 9 \div (4^2 \div 2) = -\frac{1}{8}$

7)   Choice D is correct.

Write the proportion and solve for missing side.

$\frac{\text{Smaller triangle height}}{\text{Smaller triangle base}} = \frac{\text{Bigger triangle height}}{\text{Bigger triangle base}} \Rightarrow \frac{80cm}{200cm} = \frac{80 + 460cm}{x} \Rightarrow x = 1,350\ cm$

8)   Choice A is correct.

For each option, choose a point in the solution part and check it on both inequalities.

$y \leq x + 4$
$2x + y \leq -4$

A.   Point $(-4, -4)$ is in the solution section. Let's check the point in both inequalities.

   $-4 \leq -4 + 4$, It works

   $2(-4) + (-4) \leq -4 \Rightarrow -12 \leq -4$, it works (this point works in both)

B.   Let's choose this point $(0, 0)$
       $0 \leq 0 + 4$, It works
       $2(0) + (0) \leq -4$, That's not true!

C.   Let's choose this point $(-5, 0)$
       $0 \leq -5 + 4$, That's not true!

D.   Let's choose this point $(0, 5)$
       $5 \leq 0 + 4$, That's not true!

9)   Choice B is correct

The ratio of boy to girls is $3:5$. Therefore, there are 3 boys out of 8 students. To find the answer, first divide the total number of students by 8, then multiply the result by 3.
$600 \div 8 = 75 \Rightarrow 75 \times 3 = 225$

10) Choice D is correct

$90 \div \frac{1}{9} = 90 \times 9 = 810$

11) **Choice B is correct.**

Translated 5 units down and 4 units to the left means: $(x.y) \Rightarrow (x - 4, y - 5)$

12) Choice A is correct

Area of a rectangle $= width \times height, Area = 148 \times 90 = 1,3320 \ sq.ft$

13) Choice C is correct.

$\frac{4}{23} = 0.173$ and $25\% = 0.25$ therefore x should be between 0.173 and 0.25. Only choice B $(\sqrt{0.044}) = 0.20$ is between 0.173 and 0.25.

14) Choice D is correct

Some of prime numbers are: $2, 3, 5, 7, 11, 13$. Find the product of two consecutive prime numbers: $2 \times 3 = 6$ (not in the options), $3 \times 5 = 15$ (bingo!), $5 \times 7 = 35$ (not in the options)

15) Choice B is correct

The perimeter of the trapezoid is $36 \ cm$.

Therefore, the missing side (height) is $= 36 - 8 - 12 - 6 = 10 \ cm$

Area of a trapezoid: $A = \frac{1}{2} h (b_1 + b_2) = \frac{1}{2} (10)(6 + 8) = 70 \ cm^2$

16) Choice A is correct

$\frac{1}{2}$ of the distance $4\frac{1}{5}$ miles is: $\frac{1}{2} \times 4\frac{1}{5} = \frac{1}{2} \times \frac{21}{5} = \frac{21}{10}$, Converting $\frac{21}{10}$ to a mixed number gives: $\frac{21}{10} = 2\frac{1}{10}$

17) Choice B is correct

$average = \frac{sum}{total} = \frac{40 + 45 + 50}{3} = \frac{135}{3} = 45 \ miles$

18) Choice B is correct

Use Pythagorean theorem: $a^2 + b^2 = c^2 \rightarrow s^2 + h^2 = (3s)^2 \rightarrow s^2 + h^2 = 9s^2$
Subtracting s^2 from both sides gives: $h^2 = 8s^2$
Square roots of both sides: $h = \sqrt{8s^2} = \sqrt{4 \times 2 \times s^2} = \sqrt{4} \times \sqrt{2} \times \sqrt{s^2} = 2 \times s \times \sqrt{2} = 2s\sqrt{2}$

19) Choice C is correct

Let x be the number of purple marbles. Let's review the choices provided:

A. $\frac{1}{11}$, if the probability of choosing a purple marble is one out of ten, then:

$Probability = \frac{number\ of\ desired\ outcomes}{number\ of\ total\ outcomes} = \frac{x}{40+40+30+x} = \frac{1}{11}$

Use cross multiplication and solve for x. $11x = 110 + x \rightarrow 10x = 110 \rightarrow x = 11$

Since, number of purple marbles can be 9, then, choice be the probability of randomly selecting a purple marble from the bag.

Use same method for other choices.

B. $\frac{1}{6}$

$\frac{x}{40+40+30+x} = \frac{1}{6} \rightarrow 6x = 110 + x \rightarrow 5x = 110 \rightarrow x = 22$

C. $\frac{2}{5}$

$\frac{x}{40+40+30+} = \frac{2}{5} \rightarrow 5x = 220 + 2x \rightarrow 3x = 220 \rightarrow x = 73.3$

D. $\frac{1}{23}$

$\frac{x}{40+40+30+} = \frac{1}{23} \rightarrow 23x = 110 + x \rightarrow 22x = 110 \rightarrow x = 5$

Number of purple marbles cannot be a decimal.

20) Choice C is correct

Let x be the original price of the dress. Then: 23% of $x = 21.87$

$x = \frac{23}{100}x = 21.87$, $x = \frac{100 \times 21.87}{23} \cong 95.09$

21) Choice D is correct

$\frac{8}{35} = 0.228$

22) Choice B is correct

30% of A is 1,200 Then: $0.3A = 1,200 \rightarrow A = \frac{1,200}{0.3} = 4,000$

12% of 4,000 is: $0.12 \times 4,000 = 480$

23) Choice D is correct

Simplify:

$$\frac{\frac{1}{3} - \frac{x-4}{9}}{\frac{x^3}{3} - \frac{7}{3}} = \frac{\frac{1}{3} - \frac{x-4}{9}}{\frac{x^3 - 7}{3}} = \frac{3(\frac{1}{3} - \frac{x-4}{9})}{x^3 - 7}$$

$\Rightarrow$Simplify: $\frac{1}{3} - \frac{x-4}{9} = \frac{7-x}{9}$

Then: $\frac{3(\frac{7-x}{9})}{x^3 - 7} = \frac{\frac{7-x}{3}}{x^3 - 7} = \frac{7-x}{3(x^3 - 7)} = \frac{7-x}{3x^3 - 21}$

24) Choice A is correct

$(6.2 + 8.3 + 2.4) \times x = x$, $16.9x = x$, Then: $x = 0$

25) Choice B is correct

For sum of 5: $(1 \,\&\, 4)$ *and* $(4 \,\&\, 1)$, $(2 \,\&\, 3)$ and $(3 \,\&\, 2)$, therefore we have 4 options.
For sum of 8: $(5 \,\&\, 3)$ *and* $(3 \,\&\, 5)$, $(4 \,\&\, 4)$ and $(2 \,\&\, 6)$, $(6 \,\&\, 2)$, we have 5 options. To get a sum of 5 or 8 for two dice: $4 + 5 = 9$
Since, we have $6 \times 6 = 36$ total number of options, the probability of getting a sum of 5 and 8 is 9 out of 36 or $\frac{9}{36} = \frac{1}{4}$

26) Choice C is correct

Write a proportion and solve. $\frac{7}{38} = \frac{x}{190} \rightarrow x = \frac{7 \times 190}{38} = 35$

27) Choice B is correct

$78.56 \div 0.05 = 1{,}571.2$

28) Choice D is correct

The distance of A to B on the coordinate plane is: $\sqrt{(x_1 - x_2)^2 + (y_1 - y_2)^2} = \sqrt{(2 - 10)^2 + (6 - 12)^2} = \sqrt{8^2 + 6^2}, = \sqrt{64 + 36} = \sqrt{100} = 10$
The diameter of the circle is 10 and the radius of the circle is 5. Then: the circumference of the circle is: $2\pi r = 2\pi(5) = 10\pi$

29) Choice C is correct

$2x^2 + 6 = 26 \rightarrow 2x^2 = 20 \rightarrow x^2 = 10 \rightarrow x = \pm \sqrt{10}$

30) Choice A is correct

Diameter $= 20$, then: Radius $= 10$, Area of a circle $= \pi r^2 \Rightarrow A = 3.14(10)^2 = 314$

31) Choice A is correct

$6 \, days \, 20 \, hours \, 36 \, minutes - 4 \, days \, 12 \, hours \, 24 \, minutes = $
$2 \, days \, 8 \, hours \, 12 minutes$

32) Choice C is correct

Formula of triangle area $= \frac{1}{2}(base \times height)$. Since the angles are $45 - 45 - 90$, then this is an isosceles triangle, meaning that the base and height of the triangle are equal.
$Triangle \, area = \frac{1}{2}(base \times height) = \frac{1}{2}(4 \times 4) = 8 \, square \, feet$

33) Choice B is correct

The mean of the data is 11. Then: $\frac{x+10+15+13+6}{5} = 11 \rightarrow x + 44 = 55 \rightarrow x = 55 - 44 = 11$

34) Choice C is correct

The difference of the file added, and the file deleted is:
$542,159 - 499,986 = 42,173$ bytes
$837,036 + 42,173 = 879,209$ bytes

35) Choice B is correct

$40\% \ of \ 70 = 28 \rightarrow 70 + 28 = 98$

36) Choice D is correct

$x^{\frac{1}{2}}$ equals to the root of x. Then: $12 + x^{\frac{1}{2}} = 24 \rightarrow 12 + \sqrt{x} = 24 \rightarrow \sqrt{x} = 12 \rightarrow x = 144$
$x = 144$ and $5 \times x$ equals: $5 \times 144 = 720$

37) Choice C is correct

Only choice C represents the statement "twice the difference between 5 times H and 2 gives 35". $2(5H - 2) = 35$

38) Choice D is correct

The area of the circle is $25\pi \ cm^2$, then, its diameter is $10cm$. $area \ of \ a \ circle = \pi r^2 = 25\pi \rightarrow r^2 = 25 \rightarrow r = 5 \ cm$ .Radius of the circle is 5 and diameter is twice of it, 10.One side of the square equals to the diameter of the circle. Then: $Area \ of \ square = side \times side = 10 \times 10 = 100 \ cm^2$

39) Choice C is correct.

When a point is reflected over x axes, the (y) coordinate of that point changes to $(-y)$ while its x coordinate remains the same. C $(9,7) \rightarrow$ C' $(9,-7)$

40) Choice D is correct.

A set of ordered pairs represents y as a function of x if: $x_1 = x_2 \rightarrow y_1 = y_2$
In choice A: $(5,-2)$ and $(5,7)$ are ordered pairs with same x and different y, therefore y isn't a function of x.
In choice B: $(2,2)$ and $(2,7)$ are ordered pairs with same x and different y, therefore y isn't a function of x.
In choice C: $(8,7)$ and $(8,18)$ are ordered pairs with same x and different y, therefore y isn't a function of x.

41) Choice D is correct

If the length of the box is $24 \ cm$, then the width of the box is one third of it, $8 \ cm$, and the height of the box is $4 \ cm$ (half of the width). The volume of the box is:
$V = length \times width \times height = (24)(8)(4) = 768 \ cm^3$

42) Choice D is correct

Number of squares equal to: $\frac{40 \times 12}{4 \times 4} = 10 \times 3 = 30$

43) Choice A is correct

David's weekly salary is $230 plus 9% of $1,200. Then: $9\% \ of \ 1,200 = 0.09 \times 1,200 = 108$
$230 + 108 = 338$

44) Choice B is correct

$5x^3y^2 + 4x^5y^3 - (6x^3y^2 - 4xy^5) = 5x^3y^2 + 4x^5y^3 - 6x^3y^2 + 4xy^5)$
$$= 4x^5y^3 - x^3y^2 + 4xy^5$$

45) Choice B is correct

Let P be circumference of circle A, then; $2\pi r_A = 20\pi \rightarrow r_A = 10$
$r_A = 5r_B \rightarrow r_B = \frac{10}{5} = 2 \rightarrow$ Area of circle B is; $\quad \pi r_B^2 = 4\pi$

46) Choice D is correct

The area of the square is 64 square inches. $Area \ of \ square = side \times side = 8 \times 8 = 64 \ inch^2$
The length of the square is increased by 5 inches and its width decreased by 4 inches. Then, its area equals: $Area \ of \ rectangle = width \times length = 13 \times 4 = 52$
The area of the square will be decreased by 12 square inches. $64 - 52 = 12$

47) Choice D is correct

Write a proportion and solve. $\frac{3}{2} = \frac{x}{80}$, Use cross multiplication: $2x = 240 \rightarrow x = 120$

ISEE Upper Level Math Practice Test 4

Quantitative Reasoning

1) Choice C is correct

$(4x + 9) - (4x - 3) = 4x - 4x + 9 + 3 = 12$

2) Choice B is correct

Find the value of each choice:
$2 \times 2 \times 5 \times 5 = 100$
$2 \times 2 \times 2 \times 5 \times 5 \times 7 = 1,400$
$2 \times 7 = 14$

$2 \times 2 \times 2 \times 5 \times 7 = 280$

3) Choice D is correct

Write a proportion and solve. $\frac{6i}{150feet} = \frac{20in}{x} \rightarrow x = \frac{150 \times 20}{6} = 500 \; feet$

4) Choice A is correct

Let x be all expenses, then $\frac{22}{100} x = \$550 \rightarrow x = \frac{100 \times \$550}{22} = \$2,500$

He spent for his rent: $\frac{27}{100} \times \$2,500 = \$675$

5) Choice A is correct

Area of the circle is less than 14π. Use the formula of areas of circles. $Area = \pi r^2 \Rightarrow 49 \pi > \pi r^2 \Rightarrow 49 > r^2 \Rightarrow r < 7$.Radius of the circle is less than 7. Let's put 7 for the radius. Now, use the circumference formula: $Circumference = 2\pi r = 2\pi (7) = 14 \pi$.Since the radius of the circle is less than 7. Then, the circumference of the circle must be less than 14π. Only choice A is less than 14π

6) Choice C is correct

Recall that the formula for the average is: $Average = \frac{sum \; of \; data}{number \; of \; data}$

First, compute the total weight of all balls in the basket: $35g = \frac{total \; weight}{25 \; balls}$
$35g \times 25 = total \; weight = 875g$

Next, find the total weight of the 5 largest marbles: $50g = \frac{total \; weigh}{5 \; marbles}$
$50 \; g \times 5 = total \; weight = 250 \; g$

The total weight of the heaviest balls is $250 \; g$. Then, the total weight of the remaining 20 balls is $625g$.$875 \; g - 250 \; g = 625 \; g$.

The average weight of the remaining balls: $Average = \frac{625 \; g}{20 \; marbles} = 31.25g$ per ball

7) Choice C is correct

The smallest possible value of $f(x)$ will occur when $x = 0$. Since x^2 is always positive, any positive or negative value of x will make the value of $f(x)$ greater than 6. Substitute 0 for x and evaluate the expression: $f(0) = (0)^2 + 6 = 6$

8) Choice D is correct

There is not enough information to determine the answer of the question. An average speed represents a distance divided by time and it does not provide information about the speed at specific time. Alice could drove exactly 45 miles per hour from start to finish, or she could drive 65 miles per hour for half of distance and 45 miles per hour for the other half.

9) Choice D is correct

There are 2 sets of values, one set from 1 to n, and the other set from $n + 1$ to $2n$. Since the second set begins immediately after the first set, the two sets can be combined. The sum of the positive integers from 1 to $2n$ inclusive is equal to the sum of the positive integers from 1 to n plus the sum of the positive integers from $n + 1$ to $2n$: $3,350 + 4,866 = 8,216$

10) Choice C is correct

The percentage discount is the reduction in price divided by the original price. The difference between original price and sale price is: $14.65 − $8.34 = $6.31
The percentage discount is this difference divided by the original price: $6.31 ÷ $14.65 ≅ 0.43
Convert the decimal to a percentage by multiplying by 100%: 0.43 × 100% = 43%

11) Choice C is correct

Let's review the choices provided:

A. Number of books sold in April is: 480

Number of books sold in July is: 960 → $\frac{480}{960} = \frac{48}{96} = \frac{1}{2}$

B. number of books sold in July is: 960

Half the number of books sold in May is: $\frac{1,360}{2} = 680 \to 960 > 680$

C. number of books sold in June is: 240

Half the number of books sold in April is: $\frac{480}{2} = 240 \to 240 = 240$

D. $480 + 240 = 720 < 960$

Only choice C is correct.

12) Choice D is correct

The median of a set of data is the value located in the middle of the data set. Combine the 2 sets provided, and organize them in ascending order: $\{2, 4, 5, 7, 9, 11, 13, 15, 16, 18\}$

Since there are an even number of items in the resulting list, the median is the average of the two middle numbers. $Median = (9 + 11) \div 2 = 10$

13) Choice D is correct

If 17 balls are removed from the bag at random, there will be one ball in the bag. The probability of choosing a brown ball is 1 out of 19. Therefore, the probability of not choosing a brown ball is 17 out of 19 and the probability of having not a brown ball after removing 17 balls is the same.

14) Choice D is correct

Let x be the number of current stamps in the collection. Then: $\frac{4}{3}x - x = 150 \to \frac{1}{3}x = 150 \to$
$x = 450$, 40% more of 450 is: $450 + 0.40 \times 450 = 450 + 180 = 630$

15) Choice B is correct

$(x^2 - y^2) = (x - y)(x + y)$, Then: $x^2 - y^2 = 7 \times 6 = 42$

16) Choice A is correct

The formula for the area of a rectangle is: $Area = Width \times Length$
It is given that $L = 3W$ and that $A = 108$. Substitute the given values into our equation and solve for W: $108 = w \times 3w \to 108 = 3w^2 \to w^2 = 36 \to w = 6$
It is given that $L = 3W$, therefore, $L = 3 \times 6 = 18$
The perimeter of a rectangle is: $2L + 2W$, Perimeter = $2 \times 18 + 2 \times 6$, Perimeter = 48

17) Choice D is correct

The ratio of boy to girls is $7:4$. Therefore, there are 7 boys out of 11 students. To find the answer, first divide the total number of students by 11, then multiply the result by 7.
$55 \div 11 = 5 \Rightarrow 5 \times 7 = 35$. There are 35 boys and 20 $(55 - 35)$ girls. So, 15 more girls should be enrolled to make the ratio $1:1$

18) Choice D is correct

The sum of 8 numbers is greater than 320 and less than 480. Then, the average of the 8 numbers must be greater than 40 and less than 60.
$$\frac{320}{8} < x < \frac{480}{8} \to 40 < x < 60$$
The only choice that is between 40 and 60 is 45.

19) Choice D is correct

Let x be number of gallons the tank can hold when it is full. Then: $\frac{5}{2}x = 35 \to x = \frac{2}{5} \times 35 = 14$

20) Choice B is correct

If two triangles are similar, then the ratios of corresponding sides are equal.
$\frac{AC}{AE} = \frac{BC}{DE} = \frac{20}{10} = 2 , \frac{AC}{AE} = 2$
This ratio can be used to find the length of AC: $AC = 2 \times AE$
$AC = 2 \times 10 \to AC = 20$
The length of AE is given as 10 and we now know the length of AC is 20, therefore:
$EC = AC - AE , EC = 20 - 10, \quad EC = 10$

21) Choice B is correct

In order to solve for the variable b, first take square roots on both sides: $\sqrt{f} = \frac{cz}{b}$, then multiply both sides by b: $b\sqrt{f} = cz$. Now, divide both sides by $\sqrt{f}$: $\qquad b = \frac{cz}{\sqrt{f}}$

22) Choice A is correct

Column A: $5^2 = 25$, Column B: $\sqrt[3]{125} = 5$ (recall that $5^3 = 125$)

23) Choice B is correct

A number raised to the exponent $(\frac{1}{2})$ is the same thing as evaluating the square root of the number. Therefore: $(52)^{\frac{1}{2}} = \sqrt{52}$
Since $\sqrt{49}$ is smaller than $\sqrt{52}$, column A $(\sqrt{49} = 7)$ is smaller than $\sqrt{52}$.

24) Choice A is correct

The average is the sum of all terms divided by the number of terms. $21 + 29 + 37 = 87$,
$87 \div 3 = 29$, This is greater than 28.

25) Choice B is correct

Since both columns have 435 as a factor, we can ignore that number.

$16 \times 25 = 400$, $19 \times 22 = 418$, Column B is greater.

26) Choice D is correct

Since x is an integer and can be positive and negative, then the relationship cannot be determined from the information given. Let's choose some values for x.

$x = 1$, then the value in column A is smaller. $-1 < \frac{1}{3}$

Let's choose a negative value for x. $x = -1$, then the value in column A is greater.

$1 > \frac{-1}{3} \to 1 > -\frac{1}{3}$

27) Choice C is correct

To raise a quantity to a negative power, invert the numerator and denominator, and then raise the base to the indicated power. Therefore:

$(\frac{4}{1})^{-3} = (\frac{1}{4})^3$, The Columns are the same value.

28) Choice A is correct

First, simplify the inequality: $3x + 7 > x - 1 \to 3x - x > -1 - 7 \to 2x > -8 \to x > -4$

29) Choice A is correct

First, find the values of x in both columns.

Column A: $8|3x - 2| = 16 \to |3x - 2| = 2$

$3x - 2$ can be 2 or -2.

$3x - 2 = 2 \to 3x = 4 \to x = \frac{4}{3}$

$3x - 2 = -2 \to 3x = 0 \to x = 0$

Column B: $8|3x + 2| = 16 \to |3x + 2| = 2$

$3x + 2$ can be 2 or -2.

$3x + 2 = 2 \to 3x = 0 \to x = 0$

$3x + 2 = -2 \to 3x = -4 \to x = -\frac{4}{3}$

The greatest value of x in column A is $\frac{4}{3}$ and the greatest value of x in column B is 0.

30) Choice D is correct

Simplify both columns.

Column A: $(x)^5(x)^2 = x^7$

Column B: $(x^5)^2 = x^{10}$

Column A evaluates to x^7 and Column B evaluates to x^{10}. In the case where $x = 0$, the two columns will be equal, but if $x = 2$, the two columns will not be equal. Consequently, the relationship cannot be determined.

31) Choice D is correct

The probability that an event will occur + the probability that that event will NOT occur must equal 1. Since we don't have any numerical information about the probability, it is possible that the probability that event x occurs is 25%, 50% or any other percent. The probability that event

x will not occur will always be 100% minus the probability that event x does occur. Because both columns can exhibit a range of values, the relationship cannot be determined.

32) Choice A is correct

Let x be the original price of the sport jacket. The selling price of a sport jacket including 20% discount is $68. Then: $x - 0.20x = 68 \rightarrow 0.80x = 68 \rightarrow x = \frac{68}{0.80} = 85$

The original price of the jacket is $85 which is greater than column B ($80).

33) Choice D is correct

Factor the expression if possible. Begin by moving all terms to one side before factoring:
$x^2 - 2x - 20 = 15$
$x^2 - 2x - 35 = 0$
To factor this quadratic, find two numbers that multiply to -35 and sum to -2:
$(x - 7)(x + 5) = 0$
Set each expression in parentheses equal to 0 and solve: $x - 7 = 0$
$x = 7$, $x + 5 = 0$, $x = -5$
Quadratic equations can have TWO possible solutions. Since one of these is greater than 5 and one of them is less than 5, we cannot determine the relationship between the columns.

34) Choice B is correct

Recall that numbers between 0 and 1 when raised to power of positive integers become smaller.
For example, $(0.5)^2 = 0.25$.
Then: $(0.82)^{27} > (0.82)^{28}$

35) Choice B is correct

Because of the word "and" the events described in each column must be calculated separately and then multiplied: For column A: Probability of rolling a 4: $\frac{1}{6}$

Probability of getting heads: $\frac{1}{2}$, $\frac{1}{6} \times \frac{1}{2} = \frac{1}{12}$

For column B: Probability of an odd number: $\frac{3}{6} = \frac{1}{2}$

Probability of getting a spade: $\frac{13}{52} = \frac{1}{4}$, $\frac{1}{2} \times \frac{1}{4} = \frac{1}{8}$

Since $\frac{1}{8}$ is a larger number than $\frac{1}{12}$, Colum B is greater

36) Choice A is correct

Sum of one quarter, three nickels, and three pennies is: $\$0.25 + 3\,(\$0.05) + \$0.03 = \$0.43$

37) Choice A is correct

Let's consider the properties of odd and even integers:
$Odd +/- Odd = Even$
$Even +/- Even = Even$
$Odd +/- Even = Odd$

$Odd \times Odd = Odd$
$Even \times Even = Even$
$Odd \times Even = Even$
Now let's review the columns.
For column A: $x(x + y)$
$(odd)(odd + even)$
$(odd)(odd)$
(odd)
For Column B:
$(x - y) - y^2$
$(odd - even) - (even)^2$
$(odd) - (even)(even)$
$(odd) - (even)$
(odd)
Since an odd number is considered greater according to the problem statement, the answer is A.

ISEE Upper Level Math Practice Test 4

Mathematics Achievement

1) Choice D is correct.

Plug in each pair of numbers in the equation. The answer should be 20.

A. $(2, 1)$: $4(2) + 6(1) = 14$ No!
B. $(-1, 3)$: $4(-1) + 6(3) = 14$ No!
C. $(-2, 2)$: $4(-2) + 6(2) = 4$ No!
D. $(2, 2)$: $4(2) + 6(2) = 20$ Yes!

2) Choice D is correct

Let x be the integer. Then: $2x - 5 = 91$, Add 5 both sides: $2x = 96$, Divide both sides by 2: $x = 48$.

3)   Choice A is correct

First, multiply both sides of inequality by 5. Then: $\frac{|3+x|}{5} \leq 8 \rightarrow |3 + x| \leq 40$

$-40 \leq 3 + x \leq 40 \rightarrow -40 - 3 \leq x \leq 40 - 3 \rightarrow -43 \leq x \leq 37$

4)   Choice B is correct

Subtract $\frac{1}{5b}$ and $\frac{1}{b^2}$ from both sides of the equation. Then: $\frac{1}{5b^2} + \frac{1}{5b} = \frac{1}{b^2} \rightarrow \frac{1}{5b^2} - \frac{1}{b^2} = -\frac{1}{5b}$

Multiply both numerator and denominator of the fraction $\frac{1}{b^2}$ by 5. Then: $\frac{1}{5b^2} - \frac{5}{5b^2} = -\frac{1}{5b}$

Simplify the first side of the equation: $-\frac{4}{5b^2} = -\frac{1}{5b}$

Use cross multiplication method: $20b = 5b^2 \rightarrow 20 = 5b \rightarrow b = 4$

5) Choice A is correct

The sum of supplement angles is $180°$. Let x be that angle. Therefore, $x + 9x = 180°$ $10x = 180°$, divide both sides by 10: $x = 18°$

6) Choice B is correct

$x\% \, 26 = 1.3 \rightarrow \frac{x}{100} 26 = 1.3 \rightarrow x = \frac{1.3 \times 100}{26} = 5$

7) Choice B is correct

Plug in the value of $x = 20$ into both equations. Then: $C(x) = x^2 + 2x = (20)^2 + 2(20) = 400 + 40 = 440, R(x) = 40x = 40 \times 20 = 800, 800 - 440 = 360$, So, the profit is $360.

8) Choice C is correct

$7x^3y^3(2x^3y)^3 = 7x^3y^3(8x^9y^3) = 56x^{12}y^6$

9) Choice D is correct

From choices provided, only choice D is correct. $E = 5 + A, A = S - 4$

10) Choice A is correct

Use Pythagorean Theorem: $a^2 + b^2 = c^2 \Rightarrow 4^2 + 3^2 = c^2 \Rightarrow 25 = c^2 \Rightarrow c = 5 \, cm$

11) Choice C is correct

$24 \, hours = 86,400 \, seconds, 1,520 \, minutes = 91,200 \, seconds$
$3 \, days = 72 \, hours = 259,200 \, seconds$

12) Choice C is correct

$C = 2\pi r \Rightarrow C = 2\pi \times 5 = 10\pi \Rightarrow \pi = 3.14 \rightarrow C = 10\pi = 31.4$ inches

13) Choice C is correct

Let's review the choices provided:
A. $(6 \times 10^3) + (2 \times 10^2) + (3 \times 10) = 6,000 + 200 + 30 = 6,230$
B. $(6 \times 10^2) + (2 \times 10^1) - 5 = 600 + 20 - 5 = 615$
C. $(6 \times 10^2) + (2 \times 10^1) + 3 = 600 + 20 + 3 = 623$
D. $(6 \times 10^1) + (2 \times 10^2) + 3 = 60 + 200 + 3 = 263$
Only choice C equals to 623.

14) Choice B is correct

First draw an isosceles triangle. Remember that two sides of the triangle are equal.
Let put a for the legs. Then: Use Pythagorean theorem to find the value of a:
$a^2 + b^2 = c^2 \rightarrow a^2 + a^2 = 8^2$

Isosceles right triangle
Simplify: $2a^2 = 64 \rightarrow a^2 = 32 \rightarrow a = \sqrt{32}$
$a = \sqrt{32} \Rightarrow$ area of the triangle is $= \frac{1}{2}(\sqrt{32} \times \sqrt{32}) = \frac{1}{2} \times 32 = 16 \ cm^2$

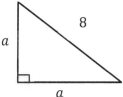

15) Choice C is correct

$\frac{5}{500} = \frac{x}{860} \Rightarrow x = \frac{5 \times 860}{500} = \$ 8.6$

16) Choice B is correct

Area of a circle equals: $A = \pi r^2$, The new diameter is 20% larger than the original then the new radius is also 20% larger than the original. 20% larger than r is $1.2r$. Then, the area of larger circle is: $A = \pi r^2 = \pi(1.2r)^2 = \pi(1.44r^2) = 1.44\pi r^2$.
$1.44\pi r^2$ is 44% bigger than πr^2.

17) Choice B is correct

$89.44 \div 0.05 = 1,788.8$

18) Choice A is correct

The area of the non-shaded region is equal to the area of the bigger rectangle subtracted by the area of smaller rectangle. Area of the bigger rectangle $= 14 \times 18 = 252$
Area of the smaller rectangle $= 9 \times 3 = 27$, Area of the non-shaded region $= 252 - 27 = 225$

19) Choice D is correct

$2\frac{1}{2} - 1\frac{5}{4} =$, Break off 1 from 2: $2\frac{1}{2} = 1\frac{3}{2}$
$1\frac{3}{2} - 1\frac{5}{4} =$ Subtract whole numbers: $1 - 1 = 0$, Combine fractions: $\frac{3}{2} - \frac{5}{4} = \frac{1}{4}$

20) Choice D is correct

To find the maximum value of y, the expression $(x - 2)^2$ must be equal to 0. Because it has a negative sign. Since $x - 2$ is to the power of 2, it cannot be negative. To get 0 for the expression $(x - 2)^2$, x must be 2. Plug in 2 for x in the equation: $y = -(x - 2)^2 + 7 \rightarrow y = -(2 - 2)^2 + 7 = 7$, The maximum value of y is 7.

21) Choice B is correct

$\begin{cases} -3x - y = -5 \\ 5x - 5y = 15 \end{cases} \Rightarrow$ Multiplication (-5) in first equation $\Rightarrow \begin{cases} 15 + 5y = 25 \\ 5x - 5y = 15 \end{cases}$
Add two equations together $\Rightarrow 20x = 40 \Rightarrow x = 2$ \qquad then: $y = -1$

22) Choice C is correct

Let's review the choices provided. Put the values of x and y in the equation.

A. $(2, 7)$ $\Rightarrow x = 1 \Rightarrow y = 7$ This is true!

B. $(-2, -13)$ $\Rightarrow x = -2 \Rightarrow y = -13$ This is true!

C. $(4, 21)$ $\Rightarrow x = 4 \Rightarrow y = 17$ This is not true!

D. $(-4, -23)$ $\Rightarrow x = 2 - 4 \Rightarrow y = -23$ This is true!

23) Choice C is correct

To find total number of miles driven by Ed that week, you only need to subtract 53,431 from 52,806. $53,431 - 52,806 = 625 \ miles$

24) Choice A is correct

First draw an isosceles triangle. Remember that two sides of the triangle are equal.

Let put a for the legs. Then: Isosceles right triangle

$a = 4 \Rightarrow$ area of the triangle is $= \frac{1}{2}(4 \times 4) = \frac{16}{2} = 8 \ cm^2$

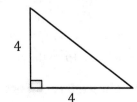

25) Choice A is correct

Factor each trinomial $x^2 - 5x + 6$ and $x^2 - 6x + 8$

$x^2 - 5x + 6 \Rightarrow (x - 2)(x - 3)$, $x^2 - 6x + 8 \Rightarrow (x - 2)(x - 4)$

The common factor of both expressions is $(x - 2)$.

26) Choice C is correct

$$
\begin{array}{r}
36 \ \text{hr.} \ \ 38 \ \text{min.} \\
- \ 23 \ \text{hr.} \ \ 25 \ \text{min.} \\
\hline
13 \ \text{hr.} \ \ 13 \text{min}
\end{array}
$$

27) Choice B is correct

$\frac{14}{26} = 0.538 \cong 0.54$

28) Choice C is correct

$x + y = 10$, Then: $9x + 9y = 9(x + y) = 9 \times 10 = 90$

29) Choice C is correct

First, convert all measurement to foot. One foot is 12 inches. Then: 12 inches $= \frac{10}{12} = \frac{5}{6}$ feet

The volume flower box is: length × width × height = $2 \times \frac{5}{6} \times 2 = \frac{10}{3}$ cubic feet.

30) Choice A is correct

$\frac{460}{20} = 23$ miles per gallon

31) Choice D is correct

$\dfrac{x^3}{15}$ $\Rightarrow$ reciprocal is : $\dfrac{15}{x^3}$

32) Choice B is correct

Let's write equations based on the information provided:
$Michelle = Karen - 9$
$Michelle = David - 4$
$Karen + Michelle + David = 91$
$Karen - 9 = Michelle \Rightarrow Karen = Michelle + 9$
$Karen + Michelle + David = 91$
Now, replace the ages of Karen and David by Michelle. Then:
$Michelle + 9 + Michelle + Michelle + 4 = 91$
$3Michelle + 13 = 91 \Rightarrow 3Michelle = 91 - 13$
$3Michelle = 78$
$Michelle = 26$

33) Choice C is correct

Use interest rate formula: $Interest = principal \times rate \times time = 1,400 \times 0.06 \times 1 = \$84$

34) Choice D is correct

$A = bh,$ $A = 3 \times 3.2 = 9.6$ square feet

35) Choice D is correct

Ellis travels $\dfrac{5}{3}$ of 90 hours. $\dfrac{5}{3} \times 90 = 150$, Ellis will be on the road for 150 hours.

36) Choice A is correct

Plug in the values of x and y in the expression:
$2x^2(y + 4) = 2(0.5)^2(5 + 4) = 2(0.25)(9) = 4.5$

37) Choice B is correct.

To find the area of the shaded region subtract smaller circle from bigger circle.
$S_{bigger} - S_{smaller} = \pi(r_{bigger})^2 - \pi(r_{smaller})^2 \Rightarrow S_{bigger} - S_{smaller} = \pi(7)^2 - \pi(5)^2 \Rightarrow$
$49\pi - 25\pi = 24\pi \ inch^2$

38) Choice D is correct

To find the discount, multiply the number by $(100\% - rate\ of\ discount)$.
Therefore, for the first discount we get: $(500)(100\% - 25\%) = (500)(0.75)$
For the next 15% discount: $(500)(0.75)(0.85)$

39) Choice A is correct

Write a proportion and solve for the missing number. $\dfrac{40}{18} = \dfrac{5}{x} \rightarrow 40x = 18 \times 5 = 90$

$$40x = 90 \rightarrow x = \frac{90}{40} = 2.25 \, ft$$

40) Choice A is correct

The ratio of boys to girls is $7: 3$. Therefore, there are 7 boys out of 10 students. To find the answer, first divide the number of boys by 7, then multiply the result by 10.
$210 \div 7 = 30 \Rightarrow 30 \times 10 = 300$

41) Choice B is correct

$$\frac{35}{100} \times 620 = x \rightarrow x = 217$$

42) Choice C is correct
The area of a $19 \, feet \, x \, 19 \, feet$ room is 361 square feet. $19 \times 19 = 361$

43) Choice C is correct

Use FOIL (First, Out, In, Last). $(4x + 4)(x + 5) = 4x^2 + 20x + 4x + 20 = 4x^2 + 24x + 20$

44) Choice C is correct

Plug in the values of x and y in the equation: $4 \blacksquare 9 = \sqrt{4^2 + 9} = \sqrt{16 + 9} = \sqrt{25} = 5$

45) Choice A is correct

Let x be the capacity of one tank. Then, $\frac{2}{3}x = 200 \rightarrow x = \frac{200 \times 3}{2} = 300$ Liters
The amount of water in four tanks is equal to: $4 \times 300 = 1,200$ Liters

46) Choice C is correct.
To add two matrices, first we need to find corresponding members from each matrix.

$$\begin{vmatrix} 3 & 6 \\ -1 & -3 \\ -5 & -1 \end{vmatrix} + \begin{vmatrix} 2 & -1 \\ 6 & 4 \\ 1 & 3 \end{vmatrix} = \begin{vmatrix} 5 & 5 \\ 5 & 1 \\ -4 & 2 \end{vmatrix}$$

47) Choice C is correct

$$Average = \frac{\text{sum of terms}}{\text{number of terms}}$$
The sum of the weight of all girls is: $20 \times 55 = 1,100 \, kg$, The sum of the weight of all boys is: $35 \times 70 = 2,450 \, kg$, The sum of the weight of all students is: $1,100 + 2,450 = 3,550 \, kg$
$Average = \frac{3,550}{55} = 64.54 \, kg$

ISEE Upper Level Practice Test 5

Quantitative Reasoning

1) Choice D is correct

Find the value of each choice:

$2 \times 2 \times 5 \times 7 = 140, 2 \times 2 \times 2 \times 2 \times 5 \times 7 = 560, 2 \times 7 = 14, 2 \times 2 \times 2 \times 5 \times 7 = 280$

2) Choice B is correct

Recall that the formula for the average is: $Average = \frac{sum\ of\ data}{number\ of\ data}$

First, compute the total weight of all balls in the basket:

$26\ g = \frac{total\ weigh}{20\ balls}$, $26g \times 20 = total\ weight = 520\ g$

Next, find the total weight of the 5 largest marbles:

$40\ g = \frac{total\ weight}{5\ marbl}$, $40\ g \times 5 = total\ weight = 200\ g$

The total weight of the heaviest balls is $200\ g$. Then, the total weight of the remaining 15 balls is $320\ g$. $520\ g - 200\ g = 320\ g$.

The average weight of the remaining balls: $Average = \frac{320\ g}{15\ marbles} = 21.33\ g\ per\ ball$

3) Choice C is correct

$(5x + 8) - (5x - 2) = 10$

4) Choice D is correct

First calculate the number of feet that 1 inch represents: $100\ ft \div 5\ in = 20\ \frac{ft}{in}$

Then multiply this by the total number of inches: $16\ in \times 20\ \frac{ft}{in} = 320\ ft$

5) Choice D is correct

Let x be all expenses, then $\frac{22}{100}x = \$770 \rightarrow x = \frac{100 \times \$770}{22} = \$3,500$

He spent for his rent: $\frac{27}{100} \times \$3,500 = \$945$

6) Choice D is correct

There is not enough information to determine the answer the question. An average speed represents a distance divided by time and it does not provide information about the speed at specific time. Alice could drove exactly 52.5 miles per hour from start to finish, or she could drive 60 miles per hour for half of distance and 45 miles per hour for the other half.

7) Choice A

Area of the circle is less than $18\,\pi$. Use the formula of areas of circles.

$$Area = \pi r^2 \Rightarrow 81\,\pi > \pi r^2 \Rightarrow 81 > r^2 \Rightarrow r < 9$$

Radius of the circle is less than 8. Let's put 8 for the radius. Now, use the circumference formula: $Circumference = 2\pi r = 2\pi\,(9) = 18\,\pi$, Since the radius of the circle is less than 9. Then, the circumference of the circle must be less than 18π. Online choices A is less than $18\,\pi$.

8) Choice C is correct

The correct answer is (C). The percentage discount is the reduction in price divided by the original price. The difference between original price and sale price is:

$$\$12.65 - \$7.38 = \$5.27$$

The percentage discount is this difference divided by the original price:

$\$5.27 \div \$12.65 = 0.417 \cong 0.42$, Convert the decimal to a percentage by multiplying by 100%: $0.42 \times 100\% = 42\%$

9) Choice B is correct

The smallest possible value of $f(x)$ will occur when $x = 0$. Since x^2 is always positive, any positive or negative value of x will make the value of $f(x)$ greater than 4. Substitute 0 for x and evaluate the expression: $f(0) = (0)^2 + 4 = 4$

10) Choice D is correct

There are 2 sets of values, one set from 1 to n, and the other set from $n + 1$ to $2n$. Since the second set begins immediately after the first set, the two sets can be combined. The sum of the positive integers from 1 to $2n$ inclusive is equal to the sum of the positive integers from 1 to n plus the sum of the positive integers from $n + 1$ to $2n$: $2,350 + 4,356 = 6,706$

11) Choice D is correct

A. Number of books sold in April is: 260

Number of books sold in July is: $500 \rightarrow \dfrac{260}{500} \neq \dfrac{1}{2}$

B. number of books sold in July is: 500

Half the number of books sold in May is: $\dfrac{980}{2} = 490 \rightarrow 500 > 490$

C. number of books sold in June is: 240

Half the number of books sold in April is: $\dfrac{260}{2} = 130 \rightarrow 130 \neq 240$

D. $260 + 240 = 500$

Only Choice D is correct.

12) Choice D is correct

The median of a set of data is the value located in the middle of the data set. Combine the 2 sets provided, and organize them in ascending order: $\{2, 3, 5, 6, 8, 10, 12, 14, 18, 20\}$

Since there are an even number of items in the resulting list, the median is the average of the two middle numbers. Median $= (8 + 10) \div 2 = 9$

13) Choice C is correct

Let x be the number of current stamps in the collection. Then: $\frac{5}{4}x - x = 120 \rightarrow \frac{1}{4}x = 120 \rightarrow$
$x = 480$, 60% more of 480 is: $480 + 0.60 \times 480 = 480 + 288 = 768$.

14) Choice D is correct

If 11 balls are removed from the bag at random, there will be one ball in the bag. The probability of choosing a brown ball is 1 out of 18. Therefore, the probability of not choosing a brown ball is 11 out of 18 and the probability of having not a brown ball after removing 11 balls is the same.

15) Choice B is correct

$(x^2 - y^2) = (x - y)(x + y)$, Then: $x^2 - y^2 = 7 \times 5 = 35$

16) Choice C is correct

The ratio of boy to girls is $3:8$. Therefore, there are 3 boys out of 11 students. To find the answer, first divide the total number of students by 11, then multiply the result by 3.

$44 \div 11 = 4 \Rightarrow 4 \times 3 = 12$, There are 12 boys and 32 $(44 - 12)$ girls. So, 20 more boys should be enrolled to make the ratio $1:1$

17) Choice B is correct

The formula for the area of a rectangle is: $Area = Width \times Length$

It is given that $L = 5W$ and that $A = 245$. Substitute the given values into our equation and solve for W:

$245 = W \times 5W$, $245 = 5W^2$, $W^2 = 49$, $W = 7$

It is given that $L = 5W$, therefore, $L = 5 \times 7 = 35$

The perimeter of a rectangle is: $2L + 2W$, Perimeter $= 2 \times 35 + 2 \times 7$, Perimeter $= 84$

18) Choice B is correct

The sum of 8 numbers is greater than 240 and less than 320. Then, the average of the 8 numbers must be greater than 30 and less than 40. $\frac{240}{8} < x < \frac{320}{8}$

$30 < x < 40$

The only choice that is between 30 and 40 is 35.

19) Choice B is correct

In order to solve for the variable n, first take square roots on both sides:

$\sqrt{a} = \frac{cz}{n}$, then multiply both sides by n: $n\sqrt{a} = cz$, Now, divide both sides by $\sqrt{a}$: $\qquad n = \frac{cz}{\sqrt{a}}$

20) Choice B is correct

If two triangles are similar, then the ratios of corresponding sides are equal.

$\frac{AC}{AE} = \frac{BC}{DE} = \frac{14}{7} = 2, \frac{AC}{AE} = 2$, This ratio can be used to find the length of AC:

$AC = 2 \times AE , AC = 2 \times 7 , AC = 14$

The length of AE is given as 7 and we now know the length of AC is 14, therefore:

$EC = AC - AE , EC = 14 - 7, \quad EC = 7$

21) Choice C is correct

Let x be number of gallons the tank can hold when it is full. Then:

$\frac{2}{5}x = 20 \rightarrow x = \frac{5}{2} \times 20 = 50$

22) Choice A is correct

The average is the sum of all terms divided by the number of terms.

Column A $12 + 24 + 28 = 64, 64 \div 3 = 21.33$

Column B $16 + 20 + 25 = 61, 61 \div 3 = 20.33$

23) Choice A is correct

Number 756 is repeated in both columns. So, we can ignore it.

$13 \times 17 = 221, 15 \times 14 = 210$

24) Choice D is correct

Since x is an integer and can be positive and negative, then the relationship cannot be determined from the information given. Let's choose some values for x.

$x = 1$, then the value in column A is greater. $1 > \frac{1}{-3}$

Let's choose a negative value for x.

$x = -1$, then the value in column B is greater. $-1 < \frac{-1}{-3} \rightarrow -1 < \frac{1}{3}$

25) Choice A is correct

First, find the values of x in both columns.

Column A: $5|4x - 3| = 10 \rightarrow |4x - 3| = 2$

$4x - 3$ can be 2 or -2.

$4x - 3 = 2 \rightarrow 4x = 5 \rightarrow x = \frac{5}{4}$

$$4x - 3 = -2 \rightarrow 4x = 1 \rightarrow x = \frac{1}{4}$$

Column B: $5|4x + 3| = 10 \rightarrow |4x + 3| = 2$

$4x + 3$ can be 2 or -2.

$$4x + 3 = 2 \rightarrow 4x = -1 \rightarrow x = -\frac{1}{4}$$

$$4x + 3 = -2 \rightarrow 4x = -5 \rightarrow x = -\frac{5}{4}$$

The greatest value of x in column A is $\frac{5}{4}$ and the greatest value of x in column B is $-\frac{1}{4}$.

26) Choice D is correct

Simplify both columns.

Column A: $(x)^2(x)^3 = x^5$

Column B: $(x^2)^3 = x^6$

Column A evaluates to x^5 and Column B evaluates to x^6. In the case where $x = 0$, the two columns will be equal, but if $x = 2$, the two columns will not be equal. Consequently, the relationship cannot be determined.

27) Choice B is correct

Use Pythagorean Theorem to find the shortest distance between Town C and Town A:

$$a^2 + b^2 = c^2, 15^2 + 8^2 = c^2 \rightarrow 225 + 64 = c^2 \rightarrow c = 17 \; miles$$

Column B is bigger than Column A.

28) Choice A is correct

Column A: $2^2 = 4$

Column B: $\sqrt[4]{81} = 3$

29) Choice A is correct

The quantity in Column B can be simplified because fractional exponents are another way of writing roots. A number raised to the exponent (½) is the same thing as evaluating the square root of the number. Therefore: $(33)^{\frac{1}{2}} = \sqrt{33}$

Even though 33 is a prime number, and it's difficult to know the value of its square root (since it will be a decimal), we do know that 33 is between 25 and 36. The square root of 25 is 5, and the square root of 36 is 6, so the square root of 33 must be between 5 and 6. Therefore, it must be smaller than 6.

30) Choice B is correct

Let x be the original price of the sport jacket. The selling price of a sport jacket including 18% discount is $41. Then: $x - 0.18x = 41 \rightarrow 0.82x = 41 \rightarrow x = \frac{41}{0.82} = 50$

The original price of the jacket is $50 which is smaller than column B ($51).

31) Choice B is correct

We need to set up the equation to maximize the value of x to determine this answer:

$0.20 \times x < 10 , x < 10 \div 0.20 , x < 50$

The value of x has to be less than 50, which is less than Column B.

32) Choice B is correct

Because of the word "and" the events described in each column must be calculated separately and then multiplied:

For column A:

Probability of rolling a 6: $\frac{1}{6}$

Probability of getting heads: $\frac{1}{2}, \frac{1}{6} \times \frac{1}{12} = \frac{1}{12}$

For column B:

Probability of an even number: $\frac{3}{6} = \frac{1}{2}$

Probability of getting a spade: $\frac{13}{52} = \frac{1}{4}$

$\frac{1}{2} \times \frac{1}{4} = \frac{1}{8}$

The correct answer is (B), since $\frac{1}{8}$ is a larger number than $\frac{1}{12}$.

33) Choice C is correct

To raise a quantity to a negative power, invert the numerator and denominator, and then raise the base to the indicated power. Therefore: $\left(\frac{4}{1}\right)^{-2} = \left(\frac{1}{4}\right)^{2}$

The Columns are the same value.

34) Choice A is correct

For Column A, begin by expressing the profit as a percent of the cost to Liza, where the profit is \$315 and the cost is \$1350: $\frac{315}{1350} = 0.2333 \times 100 = 23.33\%$

For Column B, begin by calculating the sale price, which is equal to the cost plus the profit:

$\$1350 + \$315 = \$1665$, Next, express the profit as a percent of the sale price:

$\frac{315}{1665} = 0.1891 \times 100 = 18.91\%$, Column A is greater.

35) Choice C is correct

The value of Column A is $\frac{3}{5}$ as given.

$$\frac{x}{y} = \frac{3}{5} \rightarrow 5x = 3y \rightarrow x = \frac{3}{5}y$$

Now, replace x with $\frac{3}{5}y$ in Column B. Then:

$\frac{x+3}{y+5} = \frac{\frac{3}{5}y+3}{y+5}$, Now multiply all values in both numerator and denominator by 5.

$\frac{\frac{3}{5}y+3}{y+5} = \frac{3y+15}{5y+25}$. Now, factor both numerator and denominator. Then:

$$\frac{3y+15}{5y+25} = \frac{3(y+5)}{5(y+5)} = \frac{3}{5}$$

36) Choice C is correct

Let's consider the properties of odd and even integers:

$Odd +/- Odd = Even$

$Even +/- Even = Even$

$Odd +/- Even = Odd$

$Odd \times Odd = Odd$

$Even \times Even = Even$

$Odd \times Even = Even$

If you don't have these memorized, they are easy to prove with simple numbers such as 2 and 3: $3 + 3 = 6 , 2 + 2 = 4 , 3 + 2 = 5 , 3 \times 3 = 9 , 2 \times 2 = 4 , 3 \times 2 = 6$

Now let's analyze the columns.

For column A: $(x - y)^2 - x$

$(odd + even)^2 - odd \rightarrow (odd)^2 - odd \rightarrow (odd)(odd) - odd \rightarrow odd - odd = even$

For Column B:

$(y)(x + y) \rightarrow (even)(odd + even) \rightarrow (even)(odd) = even$

37) Choice D is correct

Very often, when presented with a quadratic equation, it is useful to factor it (if possible). Begin by moving all terms to one side before factoring:

$x^2 - 4x - 15 = 6$

$x^2 - 4x - 21 = 0$

To factor this quadratic, find two numbers that multiply to -21 and sum to -4:

$(x - 7)(x + 3) = 0$, Set each expression in parentheses equal to 0 and solve:

$x - 7 = 0 , x = 7 , x + 3 = 0 , x = -3$

Quadratic equations can have TWO possible solutions. Since one of these is greater than 0 and one of them is less than 0, we cannot determine the relationship between the columns.

ISEE Upper Level Practice Test 5
Mathematics Achievement

1) Choice B is correct

Subtract $\frac{1}{7b}$ and $\frac{1}{b^2}$ from both sides of the equation. Then:

$$\frac{1}{7b^2} + \frac{1}{7b} = \frac{1}{b^2} \rightarrow \frac{1}{7b^2} - \frac{1}{b^2} = -\frac{1}{7b}$$

Multiply both numerator and denominator of the fraction $\frac{1}{b^2}$ by 7. Then:

$$\frac{1}{7b^2} - \frac{7}{7b^2} = -\frac{1}{7b}$$

Simplify the first side of the equation: $-\frac{6}{7b^2} = -\frac{1}{7b}$

Use cross multiplication method: $42b = 7b^2 \rightarrow 42 = 7b \rightarrow b = 6$

2) Choice B is correct

First, multiply both sides of inequality by 7. Then: $\frac{|3+x|}{7} \leq 8 \rightarrow |3 + x| \leq 56$

$-56 \leq 3 + x \leq 56 \rightarrow -56 - 3 \leq x \leq 56 - 3 \rightarrow -59 \leq x \leq 53$

,Choice B is correct.

3) Choice B is correct

Plug in the value of $x = 10$ into both equations. Then:

$$C(x) = x^2 + 2x = (10)^2 + 2(10) = 100 + 20 = \$120$$

$$R(x) = 40x = 40 \times 10 = \$400,400 - 120 = \$280$$

4) Choice D is correct

$E = 7 + A , A = S - 3$

5) **Choice A is correct**

Let x be the integer. Then: $2x - 5 = 73$, Add 5 both sides: $2x = 78$, Divide both sides by 2: $x = 39$

6) **Choice D is correct.**

Plug in each pair of numbers in the equation. The answer should be 20.

A. $(2, 1)$: $4(2) + 6(1) = 14$ No!
B. $(-1, 3)$: $4(-1) + 6(2) = 8$ No!
C. $(-2, 2)$: $4(-2) + 6(2) = 4$ No!
D. $(2, 2)$: $4(2) + 6(2) = 20$ Yes!

7) **Choice B is correct**

The sum of supplement angles is 180. Let x be that angle. Therefore, $x + 4x = 180°$

$5x = 180°$, divide both sides by 5: $x = 36°$

8) **Choice B is correct**

$x\% \ 15 = 1.2, \frac{x}{100} 15 = 1.2 \rightarrow x = \frac{1.2 \times 100}{15} = 8$

9) **Choice D is correct**

Use Pythagorean Theorem: $a^2 + b^2 = c^2, 12^2 + 5^2 = c^2 \rightarrow 169 = c^2 \rightarrow c = 13 \ cm$

10) **Choice D is correct**

Simplify. $8x^2y^3(2x^2y)^3 = 8x^2y^3(8x^6y^3) = 64x^8y^6$

11) **Choice C is correct**

$22 \ hours = 79{,}200 \ seconds, 1{,}520 \ minutes = 91{,}200 \ seconds, 2 \ days = 48 \ hours = 172{,}800 \ seconds, 5200 \ seconds$

12) **Choice B is correct**

Let's review the choices provided:

A. $(5 \times 10^3) + (2 \times 10^2) + (3 \times 10) = 5{,}000 + 200 + 30 = 5{,}230$
B. $(5 \times 10^2) + (2 \times 10^1) - 5 = 500 + 20 - 5 = 515$
C. $(5 \times 10^2) + (2 \times 10^1) + 3 = 500 + 20 + 3 = 523$
D. $(5 \times 10^1) + (2 \times 10^2) + 3 = 50 + 200 + 3 = 253$

Only choice B equals to 515.

13) **Choice C is correct**

$\frac{4}{400} = \frac{x}{860}, x = \frac{4 \times 860}{400} = \$8.6$

14) **Choice D is correct**

Area of a circle equals: $A = \pi r^2$

The new diameter is 40% larger than the original then the new radius is also 40% larger than the original. 40% larger than r is $1.4r$.

Then, the area of larger circle is: $A = \pi r^2 = \pi(1.4r)^2 = \pi(1.96r^2) = 1.96\pi r^2$

$1.96\pi r^2$ is 96% bigger than πr^2.

15) Choice D is correct

$C = 2\pi r, C = 2\pi \times 6 = 12\pi, \pi = 3.14 \rightarrow C = 12\pi = 37.68$ inches

16) Choice A is correct

First draw an isosceles triangle. Remember that two sides of the triangle are equal.

Let put a for the legs. Then:

Isosceles right triangle

$a = 8 \Rightarrow$ area of the triangle is $= \frac{1}{2}(8 \times 8) = \frac{64}{2} = 32 \ cm^2$

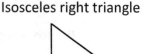

17) Choice B is correct

The area of the non-shaded region is equal to the area of the bigger rectangle subtracted by the area of smaller rectangle. Area of the bigger rectangle $= 12 \times 18 = 216$, Area of the smaller rectangle $= 10 \times 4 = 40$, Area of the non-shaded region $= 216 - 40 = 176$

18) Choice B is correct

$79.22 \div 0.04 = 1,980.5$

19) Choice D is correct

$$2\frac{2}{3} - 1\frac{5}{6} = 2\frac{4}{6} - 1\frac{5}{6} = \frac{16}{6} - \frac{11}{6} = \frac{5}{6}$$

20) Choice D is correct

Let's review the choices provided. Put the values of x and y in the equation.

A. $(1, 2)$ $\Rightarrow x = 1 \Rightarrow y = 2$ This is true!

B. $(-2, -13)$ $\Rightarrow x = -2 \Rightarrow y = -13$ This is true!

C. $(3, 12)$ $\Rightarrow x = 3 \Rightarrow y = 12$ This is true!

D. $(2, 8)$ $\Rightarrow x = 2 \Rightarrow y = 7$ This is not true!

21) Choice B is correct

To find total number of miles driven by Ed that week, you only need to subtract 39,750 from 40,128. $40,128 - 39,750 = 378$ miles

22) Choice A is correct

$$3 + (w^2 + x) = 35$$

23) Choice B is correct

$$\begin{cases} -2x - y = -9 \\ -5x - 2y = 18 \end{cases} \Rightarrow \text{Multiplication } (-2) \text{ in first equation} \Rightarrow \begin{cases} 4x + 2y = 18 \\ -5x - 2y = 18 \end{cases}$$

Add two equations together $\Rightarrow -x = 36 \Rightarrow x = -36$ then: $y = 81$

24) Choice A is correct

First draw an isosceles triangle. Remember that two sides of the triangle are equal.

Isosceles right triangle

Let put a for the legs. Then:

$a = 5 \Rightarrow$ area of the triangle is $= \frac{1}{2}(5 \times 5) = \frac{25}{2} = 12.5 \ cm^2$

25) Choice D is correct

Factor each trinomial $x^2 - 2x - 8$ and $x^2 + 6x + 8$

$x^2 - 2x - 8 \Rightarrow (x - 4)(x + 2)$, $x^2 + 6x + 8 \Rightarrow (x + 2)(x + 4)$

The common factor of both expressions is $(x + 2)$.

26) Choice B is correct

$\frac{12}{25} = 0.48$

27) Choice D is correct

$x + y = 13$, Then: $8x + 8y = 13 \times 8 = 104$

28) Choice C is correct

$$\begin{array}{r} 37 \text{ hr.} \quad 25 \text{ min.} \\ - \ 23 \text{ hr.} \quad 38 \text{ min.} \\ \hline 13 \text{ hr.} \quad 47 \text{ min.} \end{array}$$

29) Choice A is correct

$\frac{450}{18} = 25 \ miles \ per \ gallon$

30) Choice B is correct

$Perimeter \ of \ a \ rectangle = 2(width + length) = 2(89 + 55) = 288$

31) Choice D is correct

$$\frac{x^3}{12} \qquad \Rightarrow \text{reciprocal is}: \frac{12}{x^3}$$

32) Choice C is correct

Use interest rate formula:

$Interest = principal \times rate \times time = 1,300 \times 0.05 \times 1 = \$\,65$

33) Choice D is correct

Ellis travels $\frac{3}{5}$ of 80 hours. $\frac{3}{5} \times 80 = 48$. Ellis will be on the road for 48 hours.

34) Choice A is correct

$2x^2(y + 5) = 2(0.6)^2(6 + 5) = 2\,(0.36)(11) = 7.92$

35) Choice D is correct

$Michelle = Karen - 9, Michelle = David - 4, Karen + Michelle + David = 85$

$Karen - 9 = Michelle \Rightarrow Karen = Michelle + 9, Karen + Michelle + David = 85$

Now, replace the ages of Karen and David by Michelle. Then:

$Michelle + 9 + Michelle + Michelle + 4 = 85,$

$3Michelle + 13 = 85 \quad \Rightarrow \quad 3Michelle = 85 - 13$

$3Michelle = 72, Michelle = 24$

36) Choice C is correct

$A = bh, A = 2 \times 2.8 = 5.6 \; square \; feet$

37) Choice D is correct

To find the discount, multiply the number by $(100\% - rate \; of \; discount)$.

Therefore, for the first discount we get: $(200)\,(100\% - 15\%) = (200)\,(0.85)$

For the next 15% discount: $(200)\,(0.85)\,(0.85)$

38) The correct answer is B

The ratio of boys to girls is $3: 7$. Therefore, there are 3 boys out of 10 students. To find the answer, first divide the number of boys by 3, then multiply the result by 10.

$150 \div 3 = 50 \quad \Rightarrow \quad 50 \times 10 = 500$

39) Choice A is correct

Write a proportion and solve for the missing number.

$$\frac{32}{15} = \frac{6}{x} \rightarrow 32x = 6 \times 15 = 90, \ 32x = 90 \rightarrow x = \frac{90}{32} = 2.8125 \cong 2.81 \ ft$$

40) Choice B is correct.

To find the area of the shaded region subtract smaller circle from bigger circle.

$$S_{bigger} - S_{smaller} = \pi \ (r \ bigger \ )^2 - \pi \ (r \ smaller \ )^2 \Rightarrow S_{bigger} - S_{smaller}$$
$$= \pi \ (6)^2 - \pi \ (3)^2 = 36\pi - 9\pi = 27\pi \ inch^2$$

41) Choice C is correct.
To add two matrices, first we need to find corresponding members from each matrix.

$$\begin{vmatrix} 4 & 6 \\ -1 & -7 \\ -5 & -1 \end{vmatrix} + \begin{vmatrix} 0 & -1 \\ 6 & 0 \\ 2 & 3 \end{vmatrix} = \begin{vmatrix} 4 & 5 \\ 5 & -7 \\ -3 & 2 \end{vmatrix}$$

42) Choice C is correct
The area of a $17 \ feet \times 17 \ feet$ room is 289 square feet. $17 \times 17 = 289$
43) Choice C is correct

Use FOIL (First, Out, In, Last). $(3x + 4) \ (x + 5) = 3x^2 + 15x + 4x + 20 = 3x^2 + 19x + 20$

44) Choice B is correct

Plug in the values of x and y in the equation:

$$7 \blacksquare 15 = \sqrt{7^2 + 15} = \sqrt{49 + 15} = \sqrt{64} = 8$$

45) Choice A is correct

Let x be the capacity of one tank. Then, $\frac{2}{5}x = 150 \rightarrow x = \frac{150 \times 5}{2} = 375$ Liters

The amount of water in three tanks is equal to: $3 \times 375 = 1,125$ Liters

46) Choice B is correct

$$Average = \frac{sum \ of \ terms}{number \ of \ terms}$$

The sum of the weight of all girls is: $18 \times 50 = 900 \ kg$. The sum of the weight of all boys is: $32 \times 62 = 1984 \ kg$, The sum of the weight of all students is: $900 + 1984 = 2884 \ kg$

$$Average = \frac{2884}{50} = 57.68 \ kg$$

47) Choice B is correct

$$\frac{45}{100} \times 720 = x, x = 324$$

www.EffortlessMath.com

... So Much More Online!

✓ FREE Math lessons

✓ More Math learning books!

✓ Mathematics Worksheets

✓ Online Math Tutors

Need a PDF version of this book?

Please visit www.EffortlessMath.com